ACROSS AFRICA
AND ARABIA

ACROSS AFRICA AND ARABIA

Adapted from TO THE ENDS OF THE EARTH
By Irene M. Franck and David M. Brownstone

A Volume in the Trade and Travel Routes Series

Facts On File
New York • Oxford

ACROSS AFRICA AND ARABIA

Facts On File, Inc.   Facts On File Limited
460 Park Avenue South   Collins Street
New York NY 10016   Oxford OX4 1XJ
USA   United Kingdom

Library of Congress Cataloging-in-Publication Data

Across Africa and Arabia : adapted from To the ends of the earth by
  Irene M. Franck and David M. Brownstone
    p. cm. — (Trade and travel routes series)
  Includes bibliographical references.
  Summary: Discusses the development of the trade routes known as
the Nile Route, Sudan Route, Incense Road, Pilgrimage Road, and
Sahara Routes, with an overview of their social and economic history
up to the present day.
  ISBN 0-8160-1878-2
  1. Trade routes—Arabian Peninsula—History—Juvenile literature.
2. Trade routes—Africa, North—History—Juvenile literature.
3. Trade routes—Islamic countries—History—Juvenile literature.
[1. Trade routes—History.] I. Franck, Irene M. To the ends of
the earth. II. Series.
HE323.A24 1990
380.1'096—dc20   90-34176

A British CIP catalogue record for this book is available from the
British Library.

Facts On File books are available at special discounts when
purchased in bulk quantities for businesses, associations,
institutions or sales promotion. Please contact the Special
Sales Department of our New York office at 212/683-2244
(dial 800/322-8755 except in NY, AK, or HI) or in Oxford at 865/728399.

Jacket design by Catherine Hyman
Composition by Facts on File, Inc.
Manufactured by R.R. Donnelley & Sons Company
Printed in the United States of America

10 9 8 7 6 5 4 3 2 1

This book is printed on acid-free paper.

CONTENTS

LIST OF MAPS

PREFACE

Across Africa and Arabia is one volume in the Travel and Trade Routes of Human History series. The series is based on our earlier work, *To the Ends of the Earth*, published by Facts On File, Inc., in 1984. This adaption of the work for young readers has been prepared by Facts On File; many new illustrations have also been added.

Several publishers gave permission to reprint selections from their works. In this volume, the excerpts on pp. 16 and 80 are quoted from Ibn Battuta's *Travels, A.D. 1325–1354*, translated by H. A. R. Gibb, published for the Hakluyt Society by Cambridge University Press, 1958–71. The maps, drawn from *To the Ends of the Earth*, are by Dale Adams.

Irene M. Franck
David M. Brownstone

INTRODUCTION

What Is a Trade Route?

In a world without airplanes, engine-powered ships, trucks, or even paved roads, how did people journey from one place to another? How did products that were found only in a very small part of the world eventually find their way across the continents? For almost five thousand years, people have been bringing products from one part of the world to another, using trade routes. Traders from Europe, Asia, and Africa carried furs, spices, silks, pottery, knives, stone utensils, jewels, and a host of other commodities, exchanging the products found in one area for the products found in another.

When trading first began, there were no real roads. Local traders might follow trails or cross steep mountain passes in their treks from one village to another. With the passage of time, tracks might be widened and eventually paved. But the new paved roads tended to follow the old trade routes, establishing these routes as important links of communication between different cultures.

As technology advanced, sea-lanes became vital trade routes between the various continents and made possible trade with North America, South America, and Australia. Many of the highways and seaways that have been used predominantly for trade throughout history have shaped the course of history because of the many ways in which the routes have been used.

Why Study Trade Routes?

Studying the trade routes of the world is one way of learning about the history of the world. As we look at the trade routes of Europe, for example, we can see how the nations of Europe have changed throughout the centuries: we learn how Scandinavian Vikings came to sail south and west to settle in France and Britain; we can appreciate how present-day Hungary was originally settled by a wandering tribe from the Ural Mountains. In a similar way, by looking at the trade routes of Africa, we can trace the history of the slave trade and learn about the European colonization of Africa in the 18th and 19th centuries.

In addition, studying the trade routes helps us better understand the origin of many of the institutions and services with which we are familiar today. Postal systems, tolls, guidebooks, roadside restaurants, and hotels have all come into being either for service to or because of trade routes. Studying the trade routes will help you to understand how they emerged.

How to Use This Book

This book is organized in chapters. Each chapter is devoted to the history of one trade route or, in some cases, where the particular trade route has an especially long and eventful history, to a particular era in a trade route's history. Therefore, you can simply read about one trade route that particularly interests you or, alternatively, read about all the trade routes in a given area. At the end of the chapters on each route, you will find a list of books for further reading that will assist you in locating further resources should you need them to support report research or classroom work. If you are using these books as reference books for a particular history course, check the index of each to find the subject or person you need to know more about. The list of maps at the front of this book will direct you to all maps contained herein, and thereby help you to locate each trade route on the face of the earth.

Studying trade routes can be a fascinating way of learning about world history—and of understanding more about our lives today. We hope you enjoy all the volumes in the Trade and Travel Routes series.

ACROSS AFRICA
AND ARABIA

1

THE NILE ROUTE: EARLY HISTORY

THE STORY OF CIVILIZATION

The Earliest Humans. Many archaeologists believe that the first human beings on the planet evolved in east-central Africa. It was in this region that the first human civilizations developed. Since some of the first human beings evolved in Africa, some of the first trade took place among these communities. One of the prime routes for this trade was the Nile Route.

The Story of an Empire. The story of the Nile Route in its formative years is in many ways the story of the ancient empire of Egypt. Later in world history—in the seventh century A.D.— one of the world's largest religions developed in nearby Arabia (today's country of Saudi Arabia). That great religion is known as Islam.

Islam changed the history of the world. It became the basis of not one but several empires. Islam continues to be the major religion in the Middle East, Africa, and Central Asia, as well as influencing many who live in Europe, Asia, and the United States.

In Chapter 2, the rise of Islam and how it moved along the Nile Route to change the course of world history will be discussed. In this chapter, the early history of the Middle East will be explored through the history of the Nile Route—from the days of some of the world's earliest humans, through the history of the Egyptian empire, and up to the development of the Greek and Roman empires.

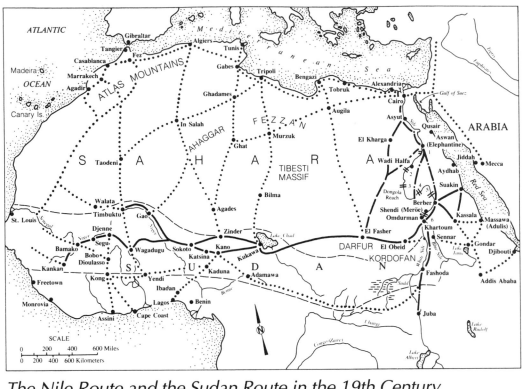

The Nile Route and the Sudan Route in the 19th Century

——— Main Sudan Routes   ······· Main Connecting Routes

— — — Derib el Arba'in (Track of the   — — — Sahel Corridor
40 days)

         =   Cataracts

—·—·— The Nile Route

THE ANCIENT ROUTES

The Nile Route. The Nile Route is the main north-south route in
East Africa. The Nile, one of the world's largest rivers, flows into
the Mediterranean Sea. Much human trade has taken place across
the Mediterranean, since it is around the Mediterranean that the
first human civilizations developed.

From the modern country of Sudan the channel of the Nile cuts
through the length of Egypt before flowing into the Mediterranean.
The course of the Nile on this section of the river is interrupted by
six waterfalls that are called *cataracts*.

Near the ancient city of Khartoum in Sudan, the Nile's two major
branches meet to form the Nile. One branch is called the Blue Nile
and it flows northwestward toward Khartoum from the Ethiopian

highlands. The Blue Nile and its main feeder stream, the Atbara, are surrounded by valleys. These valleys form part of a route farther east toward the Red Sea. The Nile's other branch is called the White Nile. The White Nile Route continues south, winding its way past great marshes of *papyrus*, a reed that early peoples used to make the first paper. This route goes south into the Kenya highlands and beyond Lake Victoria. If you follow the White Nile River far enough south you will arrive at the source of the Nile, over 4,150 miles away from the Mediterranean.

The Sudan Route. The other main travel route in East Africa is the Sudan Route, which runs east-west. The Sudan Route follows the Sahel Corridor—a strip of partly dry grassland that runs across Africa along the southern fringes of the Sahara Desert. At the east end it cuts through Ethiopia to the shores of Etritrea (a region of today's Ethiopia) on the Red Sea. This route has been a major human pathway for thousands of years.

Over the million and a half years of human evolution in Africa, the Nile Route and the Sudan Route were the main routes of migration. The first humans migrated out of Africa into other continents—the first step in the eventual populating of the whole world.

EARLY PEOPLES OF THE WORLD

The Peoples of Africa. By about 10,000 years ago, the people of the world had evolved into many different races. Many of these different races were represented in Africa. South of the Sudan and the Nile lived dark-skinned Negroid people. The Blue and White Nile regions, around the modern city of Khartoum, were occupied by Nilo-Saharans. These people were also dark-skinned but were taller and generally thinner than the Negroid people.

The rest of Africa was occupied by various peoples originally from the Arabian peninsula. These Arab peoples included Berbers living along the coastal strip of northern Africa and Cushites living in the Ethiopian highlands. The Egyptians living along the lower Nile were a mixture of Berbers and Cushites. They were the ancestors of one of the world's first empires.

Different Ways of Finding Food. The first humans were hunters and gatherers. They only knew how to get food by hunting and killing animals or by gathering vegetation that grew wild. In these early days, the Egyptians lived in forests and grasslands where they could find the food they needed for survival.

Eventually, people discovered how to keep herds of animals, such as cattle, oxen, or buffalo. These animals provided milk and could be slaughtered for meat. Their skins could be used to make blankets, clothes, and tent walls; their bones could be used to make tools.

Herding started in the Middle East around 5000 B.C. The early herders were *nomads*, or wanderers. They would drive their herds into a pasture, stay until there was no more grass for the herds to eat, and them move on. The development of herding changed not only how people lived but where they lived. The Sahel Corridor was a good place for nomadic herders to live. It was a huge area with many pastures where herds could graze.

The practice of herding spread into the Sudan by about 3000 B.C. Both the Cushites and the Nilo-Saharans adopted the herder's life. Somewhat later, the Negroid people also became herders.

The nomads generally moved north-south in the Sahel Corridor. In those days, the Sahara was not as large as it is today. It was also not as dry and desert-like. So in winter, the nomads' herds grazed near the Sahara Desert's edge. In the summer, the nomads moved their herds south toward the wetter forests near the Equator. At this time, people only traveled north-south, and there was no flow of east-west traffic along the Sudan Route.

EGYPT

The Growth of Farming. After the discovery of herding, people learned how to cultivate the land. This gave people a more constant and reliable source of food. In some parts of the world, the land is more suited to herding than to farming. But in Egypt, farming was more popular, as the land is very fertile. The valley around the Nile River is 15 miles wide, and every year it is flooded by the Nile. When the floodwaters subside, the land is covered with rich *silt*—muddy soil. This silt is very fertile and ideal for growing crops. Also, the floodwaters *irrigate*, or water, the land.

Because of these fertile conditions, Egyptians were able to take up a settled life very early. Because they could settle in one place, they built permanent villages and gave up the wandering lifestyle of the nomads. Eventually, many of these villages grew to become cities.

The First Empire. In about 3000 B.C., Upper and Lower Egypt were combined under one ruler called Menes. (Because the Nile's source is to the south, the southern part of the Nile is said to be "above" the northern part. So Upper Egypt is southern Egypt, while Lower Egypt is the part of Egypt that borders on the Mediterranean.) This early kingdom set its border at the Nile's First Cataract, just south of Elephantine Island near the modern city of Aswan. But this early kingdom reached far beyond its boundaries to communicate with many other peoples, including the Nubians.

The country of Nubia was the region between the First and Second Cataracts. The Egyptians traded with the Nubians for hardwood and ivory. Later they also traded for granite, which they used to build their great tombs and famous pyramids.

The Egyptians also sent military forces south along the Nile to collect tribute, or payments, from the people who lived in these southern regions. Sometimes the armies brought back huge numbers of prisoners and other goods from Nubia. The Pharaoh (ruler) Snefru was the ruler of Egypt at around 2700 B.C., the time when the pyramids were being built. He bragged about his campaign to Nubia: "I brought back seven thousand prisoners, and two hundred thousand cattle, large and small." The prisoners were used as slaves.

This model of a Nile boat dates from about 4,000 years ago. (Science Museum, London)

Early Boats. The Egyptians invented some early boats so that they could travel on the Nile. These early boats were apparently built from papyrus. Later Nile boats were made of Nubian hardwood. These sturdier boats could carry the heavier loads of Nubian granite needed to build the pyramids. These boats were either rowed, or moved by large poles that the sailors stuck into the bottom of the river bed, or towed by animals walking along the riverbank. Boats going upstream could sail with the northerly winds.

The Land of Punt. One of the other lands with which Egypt traded was the land of Punt on the coast of the Red Sea. Punt was very difficult for the Egyptians to reach by land because the route was blocked by the Red Sea hills and the Ethiopian highlands. So in 2800 B.C., the Egyptians began to travel to Punt by sea.

Punt had many precious goods: gold from the Red Sea hills and spices from the East, which had come to Punt via Arabia and India. These commodities were greatly desired by the Egyptians.

The Land of Yam. The Egyptians sent other expeditions southwest into the Sudan. These expeditions were carried out in *caravans*, huge parties of people and animals traveling through a desert or unfriendly area. These caravans carried enough supplies for a long trip. One caravan leader, Harkhuf, made four trips into a part of the Sudan called the land of Yam. Round trips to Yam took as long as eight months.

Eventually, camels and horses were used in caravans. But in Harkhuf's time, these animals had not yet been tamed. The pack animals he used were donkeys. On his third trip, Harkhuf took 300 donkeys—100 to carry trade goods, 100 to carry food, and 100 to carry water. The goods that Harkhuf brought back from Yam however, more than paid for the cost of the people and animals he needed to take with him. From Yam, Harkhuf brought back incense, ebony (a kind of dark wood), ivory, and leopard skins.

Attacks on Egypt. Soon after Harkhuf's journeys, Egypt became weak. This weakness was caused by Nubian and Sudanese attacks. As a result, the great cities of ancient Egypt declined, as trade with the outer world was cut off. The upset that followed is described in an ancient document from that time, the Ipuwer Papyrus:

> The palace had been overthrown. Princes are starving, the masses triumphant; noble ladies go hungry; owners of fine clothes are in rags.

Plunder and squalor are universal. Great and small say: "I wish I were dead." The harvester is robbed of his possessions. The storehouses are empty and their keepers lie dead upon the ground. There have been terrible scenes. The peasant goes out to plough, weapon in hand. People are forced to eat food that used to be given to poultry and pigs. No skilled laborers are working, for these enemies of their country have ruined their crafts. People's faces are blanched with terror for the criminals are at large. Laughter has died out of the land. The songs of the musicians have turned into a dirge. All is in ruins.

After about a century of decline, Egypt was restored under a new dynasty, based in Thebes. The Theban princes quickly moved to trade with—and control—the people of the Middle Nile. Soldiers traveled up the Nile, setting up a series of 14 forts. These forts protected river traffic and caravan routes from the attacks of nomads.

As a result of this protection, Egyptians could now trade directly with the more friendly people of Kush. Skilled Egyptian workers of all kinds—potters, jewelers, metalworkers, cabinetmakers, and others—began to settle in Kush.

But this trade route was broken by 1700 B.C. Egypt was invaded by people from western Asia, and Kush became a separate country. These invaders were called the Hyksos, and they came to rule the Nile delta (where the Nile flows into the Mediterranean).

Contributions of the Hyksos. The Hyksos made several important contributions to Egyptian culture. They brought in the horse, which they had learned to tame and which could be used for swifter travel than other animals had allowed. They also brought in the chariot, a two-wheeled cart that could be pulled quite quickly by one or more horses.

Before the Hyksos, the strongest metal that the Egyptians used was copper. The Hyksos brought in a new, stronger metal, a mixture of copper and tin known as bronze. This enabled the Egyptians to make much stronger tools and weapons. The Hyksos' bronze weapons spread from the delta up the Nile. After a century of rule by the Hyksos, the Thebans, armed with the new weapons, set up a new kingdom again in Egypt.

The New Kingdom. Under the New Kingdom, founded around 1590 B.C., Egypt was stronger than ever before. Egypt used its new strength to expand. It invaded Nubia and Kush and took control of them. It also expanded by extending trade.

Archaeologists have found Egyptian beads from this period far up the Nile, well south of the Sudd. But Egyptian traders themselves probably didn't travel so far south into Africa. They probably traded their goods to others, who in turn carried them south.

Egyptians did go farther south than they ever had before, however. For the first time, they went far enough to meet large numbers of the Negroid people. We know this, because for the first time, we see such people depicted in Egyptian art of this period. One of Egypt's rulers of the 16th century B.C., Tuthmosis I, was proud of his achievements and the travels of his people. He bragged that "his name had penetrated the whole earth."

The Nubian-built boats began to bring new trading items to Egypt: gold, ebony, ivory, ostrich feathers, fly-whisks made from giraffe tails, perfumes, oils, and some raw materials. Egyptians also brought into their country a few hundred slaves a year, taken in raids on Negroid villages farther to the south.

Besides the Nile, trade goods were still arriving by overland caravan routes from the Red Sea. And in the 15th century B.C., Queen Hatshepsut started sea trade with the land of Punt once again.

FROM KUSH TO SYRIAN RULE

The Kush Take Control. By the 13th century B.C., Egypt's central government had weakened once more. As a result, the Egyptians relied more and more on paid Nubian soldiers rather than on their own armies. They also fell into civil war. This conflict ended with the viceroy (ruler) of Kush becoming more powerful—for he was the one who had the support of the Nubian soldiers. By the 10th century B.C., Kush had won its independence from Egypt. Soon Kush began to expand its sphere of power into Egypt itself. During the 8th century B.C., its kings pushed north to the Nile delta.

The Assyrians Take Over. The Kushite reign ended within a century. Another people, the Assyrians, became dominant. They came from the east and brought with them more sophisticated weapons that were tipped with iron. The Assyrians' weapons made them the most powerful force in the area. In 671 B.C. they swarmed into the Nile Valley.

The Kushite king did not easily accept defeat. After the Assyrian victory, he staged a revolt. Then the Assyrian armies drove up the

The famous Egyptian pyramids dominated the lower Nile from very early times. (From Clara Erskine Clement, *Egypt*, 1903)

Nile, taking and sacking Thebes. This finally put an end to the reign of Kush in Egypt.

It was during these wars that camels seem to have made their first appearance in Egypt. They did not become widely used, though, since they did not breed well in the Nile Valley.

Kush Expands. The Assyrians kept control for a time, but they had overextended their troops. They could not hold all the land they had taken. Finally, they had to withdraw their troops. When they did so, the Egyptians recaptured the country for themselves. In 591 B.C., the Egyptian army won a permanent victory over the Assyrians.

Although the kingdom of Kush had been defeated, it was still relatively strong. The Kushites were able to use the knowledge of iron they had learned from the Assyrians to become stronger still.

They moved their capital to Meroë, which became the ironworking center of East Africa. During this period, the Kushites moved westward into the Sudan, at least as far as the region of Kordofan between Darfur and the Nile. Caravan routes through the Ethiopian highlands also brought Meroë into contact with the international sea traders on the Spice Route.

Kush finally became so prosperous that it had huge herds of cattle, sheep, and goats. But this wealth brought problems of its own. The herds ate too much grass, and the pastures could not grow back quickly enough. Over the centuries, the once-fertile banks of the Dongola Reach became a desert.

THE GREEK WORLD

Alexander the Great. The Greek empire built under Alexander the Great was the largest the world had ever known. It extended through Greece, Persia (today's nation of Iran), and surrounding countries. In 332 B.C., Alexander took control of Egypt, almost without a fight. Alexander chose an obscure fishing village on a western branch of the Nile's delta for his Egyptian capital. This site on the Mediterranean Sea was soon named after him—Alexandria.

Alexander went on to conquer India and Central Asia after he had taken Egypt, but he left lieutenants from his army in Egypt to rule in his name.

The Rise of the Ptolemies. After Alexander's death in 323 B.C., Egypt was ruled by a Greek general named Ptolemy. Ptolemy founded a great dynasty, known as the Ptolemaic dynasty, which ruled Egypt during the years of its greatest cultural growth. Under the Ptolemies, Alexandria grew into a major city. It attracted some of the best and brightest philosophers, who came to study in its

When the Nile flooded, it brought water and precious topsoil to Egyptian farmers in the river valley. (From James Henry Breasted, *Ancient Times: A History of the Early World...*,1914)

famous library. It was also home to one of the Seven Wonders of the World—the 600-foot-high lighthouse on the island of Pharos in Alexandria's harbor.

To the Ptolemies, the Nile and Sudan were poor and uninteresting areas. Greek traders were far more interested in the Spice Route, which began at the Red Sea. Thus, the Nile route lay relatively unused.

THE ROMAN WORLD

The Roman Empire. For many centuries, the Greek empire was the leader in the Mediterranean region. From the first century B.C., however, the Roman Empire outgrew the Greek Empire and dominated the world. As part of its growth, the Roman empire extended into Asia and the Middle East. Part of the story of how Rome conquered Egypt can be read in George Bernard Shaw's play, *Caesar and Cleopatra*, and in Shakespeare's famous play, *Antony and Cleopatra*. Rome added Egypt to its empire at the beginning of the first century B.C.

Rome and Kush. The Kushites brought themselves to Rome's attention by raiding the Egyptian city of Aswan. There they wrecked statues of the Roman emperor, Caesar Augustus. The Romans could not leave this act unpunished. They sent troops south. These troops destroyed the Kushite city of Napata and built forts in the region above the Dongola Reach to maintain military control.

In the middle of the first century A.D., the Roman emperor Nero considered expanding still further into Africa. He sent a scouting party up the Nile to see if the Sudan was worth conquering. Their report, however, was that the region was too poor and held few advantages for the Romans.

Egypt's Decline. During Roman rule, Egypt was paying heavy grain tributes to Rome. This burden sent Egypt into a decline. Villagers abandoned their homes. Irrigation systems were allowed to fall apart. People in the major cities rioted, angry about their poverty and lack of food. Upper Egypt became a target for desert raiders. Many of these raiders had once been Nile Valley farmers who lost their lands as a result of the heavy Roman demands. Even the great city of Alexandria was attacked and looted.

In the third century A.D., the Romans tried to bring peace to the Egyptian region, and paid the desert raiders to stop making raids.

The Romans continued making these payments for some time. But the raids continued. In the mid-fifth century, a Roman army was sent up the Nile Valley to fight these nomads. But the army was defeated.

Gradually, some of the desert raiders were converted to Christianity. Some Christians items were traded from person to person until they reached West Africa. Centuries later, when Europeans arrived in West Africa by sea for the first time, they found copies of these old Christian items made by the local bronzeworkers in the modern country of Ghana.

THE END OF KUSH

The Kushite city of Meroë began to decline after 350 A.D. There are no written records from the city, so no one has an accurate idea of what caused its downfall. But a written account from northern Abyssinia (today's Ethiopia) survives that gives us a good idea of what may have happened. According to this Abyssinian document, the king of a neighboring kingdom, Axum, attacked Meroë and destroyed the kingdom. The Abyssinian document said that the Axum people no longer trusted the Kushites:

> Twice and thrice they had broken their solemn oaths [promises], and had killed their neighbors without mercy, and they had stripped our deputies and messengers whom I sent to enquire into their raids, and had stolen their weapons and belongings. And as I had warned them, and they would not listen but refused to cease from their evil deeds and betook themselves to flight, I made war on them....They fled without making a stand, and I pursued them for 23 days, killing some and capturing others....I burnt their towns, both those built of bricks and those built of reeds, and my army carried off their food and copper and iron...and destroyed the statues in their temples, their granaries, and cotton trees and cast them into the river Seda [Nile].

The Kushites were pushed into the Sudan. They seem to have settled in Kordofan and Darfur. They may also have gone farther west into the Sudan—to Tibesti and Lake Chad.

2
THE NILE ROUTE: LATER HISTORY

Islam. The religion of Islam was founded in Arabia in the seventh century A.D. by a prophet named Elijah Mohammed. Islam used Christianity and Judaism as bases. Just as Christianity recognizes the prophets of Judaism, so does Islam recognize the great figures of Christianity. Adam, Noah, Abraham, Moses, and Jesus are all considered God's prophet's by Islam. The last and greatest prophet, however, is considered to be Mohammed.

The Effect of the Byzantines. In the early 600s, Egypt was under the rule of the Byzantine empire. This empire had once been the eastern half of the great Roman empire, during the time when the Romans had ruled huge portions of both Europe and Asia. Both the western and eastern parts of the Roman empire had become Christian. But their split led to a split within Christianity itself. Most Christian Europeans of the western part of the empire were Catholics, and the head of their church was the Pope, located in Rome. But Greek, Turkish, and Middle Eastern Christians in the eastern part of the empire were part of the Eastern Orthodox Church, whose ruler was the Primate, located in Constantinople.

Egypt had been part of the Byzantine empire in the early 600s and thus had been embraced by the Eastern Orthodox denomination of the Christian faith.

13

The Spread of Islam. Islam was born in the Middle East in the area that today is the country of Saudi Arabia, and it quickly spread throughout the Middle East and parts of Africa.

Only eight years after Mohammed's death in A.D. 632, Arab conquerors carried Islam into Egypt. They also quickly moved across the Red Sea to take the main Axum ports. In this process, they isolated the Christian kingdoms of Abyssinia (today's Ethiopia) and the upper Nile.

Over the next two years, the Moslem Arabs also invaded the kingdom of Nubia. They besieged the city of Old Dongola, but they could not conquer the kingdom. A treaty was eventually made with the Nubian king. The Nubians were to send 400 slaves to Aswan (which today is in Egypt) each year. The Egyptian Arabs were to send back horses, cloth, and grains, such as wheat, barley, and lentils. The peoples of the Middle Nile were also supposed to provide the Egyptian Arabs with camels.

Trade and traffic resumed on the Nile. For the next six centuries, with only a few breaks, Sudan and Egypt operated under this treaty, even though the governments that had originally agreed to it had long since vanished.

Moslem Control Expands. Like Christianity, early Islam had many major and minor *sects* or groups. Often these sects fought each other. Frequently, members of the losing sect were expelled from their homeland and had to seek refuge in foreign countries.

Egypt and the Sudan were attractive homes for many religious refugees over the centuries. These refugees converted many local people to Islam, away from their former religions. By the 10th century, many of these Moslems had colonized Nubian lands.

Moslem control continued to expand gradually through the Nile region. By the 12th century, it reached partway along the Sudan Route to Darfur. The Christians in the area were either pushed westward into the Sudan or left isolated in the mountain kingdom of Abyssinia.

MOSLEMS IN THE SUDAN

Mamelukes and Mongols. The pattern of Moslem growth was soon to be changed by events in the Sudan, Cairo, and Baghdad, where the Moslems were to suffer two major losses.

The Islamic caliphs, or rulers, did not want to lose their own areas of power, and so they maintained their own personal armies of warrior-slaves. These armies were mainly made up of Mongols or Turks and were called *Mamelukes*, or slaves. By 1250, these Mamelukes were strong enough to rise up against their masters and take control of Egypt for themselves. The Moslem rulers who had enslaved the Mamelukes now lost control of Egypt to them.

Then, in 1258, the great Moslem city of Baghdad (in today's country of Iraq) was invaded and looted by Mongol invaders from the east.

These two events greatly upset the Moslem world. Waves of refugees—many of them skilled or learned people—fled into the Sudan. As they moved, they spread the Islam religion. Most of the Christian kingdoms that were still left in the Sahel Corridor fell to the Moslems within a century. Only Abyssinia remained Christian and resisted the Moslems because it was surrounded and protected by mountains.

Two Moslem Groups Clash. By the late 14th century, the Arabs had extended their power westward to Lake Chad. There they encountered the Moslems in the kingdom of Bornu (Kanem).

The Bornuese had been converted to Islam long before and ruled from West Africa eastward almost to Darfur. They resented the new Moslem Arabs who came into their religion. They sent a written

Travelers on the Track of the Forty Days or crossing the desert loops of the Nile were always vulnerable to violent sandstorms. (From Clara Erskine Clement, *Egypt*, 1903)

complaint to the Mameluke ruler in Cairo, accusing Arabs of attacking the region and selling the captives as slaves.

The result of this clash between two Moslem groups kept the Sahel Corridor from developing into a settled trade route. Most traders didn't want to risk getting in the middle of this dispute. So most Sudanese trade went north across the Sahara.

Great Days of Traveling. The upper Nile and the Sahel Corridor may not have been great highways during this period, but the lower Nile saw a huge increase in trade and travel. We have records of the travel from that period written by the great 14th-century Arab traveler Ibn Battuta. He reported the huge numbers of people and animals that gathered in Cairo to help travelers make their caravan journey:

> In Cairo there are twelve thousand water-carriers who transport water on camels, and thirty thousand hirers of mules and donkeys, and...on its Nile there are thirty-six thousands vessels belonging to the Sultan and his subjects, which sail upstream to Upper Egypt and downstream to Alexandria and Damietta, laden with goods and commodities of all kinds.

Cairo itself was one of the greatest of all Moslem cities during this period. Ibn Battuta called it

> mother of cities and seat of the Pharoah [Egyptian ruler] the tyrant, mistress of broad provinces and fruitful lands, boundless in multitude of buildings, peerless in beauty and splendor, the meeting-place of comer and goer, the stopping-place of feeble and strong. Therein is what you will of learned and simple, grave and gay, prudent and foolish, base and noble, of high estate and low estate, unknown and famous; she surges as the waves of the sea with her throngs of folk and can scarce contain them for all the capacity of her situation and sustaining power....She has as her peculiar possession the majestic Nile.

PILGRIMAGE TO MECCA

A New Route. Many Moslems at this time journeyed to Mecca, Mohammed's birthplace, on pilgrimages. From the 14th century the pilgrims had begun to take the land route across the Sinai, because of the threats posed by the Turks to the sea routes on the Red Sea.

Then, in the early 16th century, the Turks took Egypt into their empire. The Turkish threat to the sea routes was over. At this time, however, another pilgrimage route was developed. The Sinai route out of Cairo continued to be used. But many more pilgrims began using the Sudan Route.

Shaykh 'Abjib al-Kafuta, leader of the Funj—a new Islamic empire in the middle Nile, adopted the Sudan Route first. He went northwest through the lower ranges of the Red Sea hills. Then he sailed across the Red Sea to Jidda (in today's Saudi Arabia, not far from Mecca).

Islamic holy men from the Funj empire traveled throughout the Sudan. As they reached more people, they inspired more Moslems in this area to make the pilgrimage. Often they guided the caravans themselves, bringing more and more pilgrims on the Sudan Route and then across to the Red Sea.

The Sudan Route had one great advantage over the Sahara Routes that pilgrims had previously favored. Because the Sudan was not as harsh as the Sahara Desert, pilgrims did not need to travel in such large groups. Some West African kings had traveled with thousands of servants and fellow pilgrims along the Sahara Route. Later kings used the Sudan Route—and only had to bring about 100 followers.

Poor Pilgrims. Because the Sudan Route did not demand such a difficult crossing, more people decided to make the pilgrimage to Mecca. Some people even made the trip several times.

With the increased popularity of this route came large numbers of very poor pilgrims. These were people with no money and few belongings. They traveled eastward, living on whatever alms, or donations, and earnings they could find on the way. They had to work their way along the banks of the Nile, earning the money needed to pay for the sea crossing or to join the great caravan at Cairo that led to Mecca. The Swiss traveler John L. Burckhardt describes these pilgrims as they appeared on the Nile:

> The greater part of them are quite destitute [poor], and find their way to Mecca, and back to their own country, by begging and by what they can earn by their manual labour on the road. The equipments of all these pilgrims, are exactly alike and consist of a few rags tied around the waist, a white woolen bonnet, a leather provision sack, carried on a long stick over the shoulder, a leather pouch containing the book of prayer, or a copy of a few chapters of the Koran, a wooden tablet, one foot in length by six inches in breadth, upon which they write charms, or prayers for themselves or others to learn by heart, an inkstand

Although it looks like a powerful fortress, the Cairo Citadel fell easily to Europeans. (From *Description de l'Egypte*, 1822)

formed of a small gourd, a bowl to drink out of, or to collect victuals [food] in from the charitable, a small earthen pot for ablution [washing], and a long string of beads hanging in many turns around the neck.

THE EUROPEANS EXPAND

The French, under Napoleon, became very interested in Egypt. The position of Egypt was seen as desirable by many European nations as the Isthmus of Suez (situated in Egypt) formed the link between east-west trade. Crossing the Isthmus of Suez was the shortest way east from Europe.

Napoleon Bonaparte had risen to become emperor of France and his armies had conquered most of Europe. In 1798, he set about taking the Isthmus of Suez, the key link between the Mediterranean and the Spice Routes east.

The British, wishing to stem the growth of Napoleon's empire in the east, dispatched a British fleet to Alexandria to stop the French advance. This British fleet, under the command of Admiral Horatio Nelson, arrived in Egypt before the French. Nelson asked the Egyptians to allow them to stay in the harbor, to give them supplies, and to help them against the French. But the Egyptians were suspicious of the British. They asked, "Why should you English want to fight the French in Egyptian waters when you have the whole of the Mediterranean in which to settle your differences?"

So the British left Alexandria. Then the French arrived. Their fleet of ships was so large that Egyptian observers said it "had no beginning and no end." The Egyptians sent relays of couriers (messengers) on horses up and down the banks of the Nile, warning citizens about this invasion.

The French quickly moved upstream from Alexandria on the west side of the Nile. The Egyptian army assembled to meet them. The battle they fought was known as the Battle of the Pyramids because it was fought in view of the great pyramids of the desert.

The French soldiers were not prepared for the steamy, mosquito-ridden banks of the Nile. But they were a modern army with modern weapons, and they had no trouble defeating the Egyptians within a day. The French, however, could not hold Egypt. Within three years, they were gone, beaten by Egyptian stubbornness and by the force of the British, who continued to fight the French.

Egypt had been profoundly changed by these events. The Europeans left. But an Albanian Moslem soldier, Muhammad Ali, had been sent by the Turks to fight in Egypt and to win that country back for them. He was successful but took power for himself. After his victory, he forced the Turks to name him viceroy. Muhammad Ali played a big part in making Egypt a more modern country.

The Source of the Nile

Looking for the Source. Before the 18th and 19th centuries, there was little knowledge of the upper Nile and its surrounding area. Most Africans, as well as Europeans, did not realize that the Nile had two long branches which combined to form the lower Nile—the long White Nile and the shorter but more powerful Blue Nile. And they had no idea where the Nile's source was.

James Bruce Looks for the Source. Many great explorers and adventurers were drawn to the region. One of the earliest was the Englishman James Bruce. In 1769, he landed at Massawa, seeking the source of the Nile.

Bruce moved inland to the ancient city of Axum and up into the hills of Gonder. He circled Lake Tana and found the source of the Blue Nile. But the source of the White Nile was still a mystery.

Bruce headed overland. He didn't actually try to follow the Nile as it wound its way south. Instead, he headed straight to the Funj center of Sennar. Bruce was shocked at the heat and desolation he found at Sennar:

> No horse, mule, ass, or any beast of burden, will breed, or even live at Sennar, or many miles around it. Poultry does not live there. Neither dog nor cat, sheep nor bullock, can be preserved a season there....Two greyhounds which I brought from Atbara, and the mules which I had brought from Abyssinia [Ethiopia], lived only a few weeks after I arrived.

His description of the heat in Sennar creates a vivid picture:

> I call it *hot*, when a man sweats at rest, and excessivley on moderate motion. I call it *very hot*, when a man, with thin or little clothing, sweats much, though at rest. I call it *excessively hot*, when a man in his shirt, at rest, sweats excessively, when all motion is painful, and the knees feel feeble as if after a fever. I call it *extreme hot*, when the strength fails, a disposition to faint comes on, a straitness is found round the temples, as if a small cord was drawn round the head, the voice impaired, the skin dry, and the head seems more than ordinary large and light. This, I apprehend, denotes death at hand.

Bruce felt nearly all of these stages of heat on his own trip down the Nile. From Sennar he went by camel caravan with what was left of his party to Shendi. There he found a busy caravan center close by "heaps of broken pedestals and pieces of obelisks" which he rightly deduced to be the site of ancient Meroë, the old capital of Kush.

Despite the severe heat and dryness of the area, the crossroads of the Nile and Sudan routes have always held a trading center, such as Sennar, shown here in the 19th century. (By Linant de Bellefonds, Ashmolean Museum)

Bruce then crossed the desert where the Nile begins its great winding loop southwest. He bought new camels at Berber and headed on the 400-mile desert crossing north to Aswan. By now, he only had eight people with him. And the weather was hot, even for the desert. One of his companions was literally driven crazy by the heat.

Another desert danger was the *simooms*, hot sandstorms that could blind travelers and that covered everything with sand so that it was difficult to find the route after the storm was over. Yet Bruce and his companions struggled on.

Bruce was stunned by the desert itself: "Silence, and a desperate kind of indifference about life, were the immediate effect upon us." In the end, all of the camels died, and Bruce had to leave all the baggage behind in the desert. (Later, they were able to get it back.) After 18 long, hot, sandy days, the party stumbled into Aswan. This difficult journey was not along some out-of-the-way path that Bruce found for himself. It was along one of the main Nile routes. But Bruce was totally unprepared for the rigors of desert travel.

Bruce never completed the search. Although he said he had found the source of the Nile, he was speaking about the Blue Nile. Other explorers wanted to find the source of the White Nile. The search continued.

In the 19th century, European travelers, especially English men and women like Mr. and Mrs. Samuel Baker, headed up the Nile and into the Sudan. (By Samuel Baker)

Egypt Expands into the Sudan. For years, Egyptians had been receiving gold and slaves from the Sudan. They wanted to know how to enter the Sudan and find these riches for themselves.

In 1820, Muhammed Ali sent an army up the Nile to find more slaves. For centuries, people in Africa had been captured and sold as slaves to Europeans and settlers in the Americas. Although the British Empire had outlawed the slave trade in its territories in 1807, slaves were still in demand by other nations, especially on the huge plantations in South, Central, and North America.

Ali's army was made up of mercenaries—paid soldiers who were fighting for money rather than from allegiance to Egypt. It was colorfully dressed, ranging from Turks in flashy pantaloons and slippers to Arabs in ankle-length robes. This army was poorly organized, but it did have modern weapons. People without good rifles did not have a hope of being able to defend themselves against it.

This army wiped out the few remaining Mamelukes along the Dongola Reach. Then they marched along the river to the sound of kettledrums and quickly took Shendi and Sennar. The mercenaries were paid according to the number of people they killed, so soldiers sent the ears of their dead enemies back to Cairo as proof of how many they had killed. Later armies conquered Kordofan, Darfur, and the great papyrus swamp of the Sudd. Egypt was expanding its rule.

But the Egyptians were surprised to find that the Sudan was not the rich land they had expected. The gold mines were nearly exhausted. Many slaves—sometimes half the total—died on the trip north to Cairo.

Nor was it easy for the Egyptians to rule this land. Many Sudanese fled out of their reach. Others revolted. Sudanese fighters killed the Egyptian-appointed governor at Shendi in 1822. Although Egypt was finally victorious in the eastern Sudan in 1825, the war before the victory was long and bloody. Finally, however, Egypt set up a powerful governor at Khartoum.

Egypt went beyond the Sudan to take the Sudd and the upper Nile. This was very disruptive to the people of the upper Nile. They had previously been cut off from the rest of the world by hills, swamps, and equatorial forests. They had led a sheltered life, secure in their nomadic ways. So at first, they welcomed the traders who came to them from outside their known world. They traded huge amounts of cattle and ivory for the traders' beads. Their ivory soon became a magnet for European traders and Arab merchants. But this trade and the warfare that followed disrupted the entire Sudan.

Moslem Expansion on the Sudan Route.   Changes also came to the Sudan Route. Like other parts of the Arab world in the 19th century, the Sudan was gripped by new Moslem religious movements. In the central Sudan, older religions still flourished, religions that worshipped many gods. But the new Moslem states that arose were committed to converting everyone to Islam. They were even willing to wage *jihads*, or holy wars, to do so.

   Another development in Moslem Sudan was the growing belief in the Second Coming of another Mahdi, or prophet, who would be as great as Mohammad had been. This Mahdi was supposed to appear in the east. Many Moslems headed to the eastern Sudan to wait for the Mahdi. The result was a great migration across the Sahel Corridor.

The End of the Slave Trade.   While Moslem influence was growing in the Sudan, Egypt looked more toward Europe and its customs. Great Britain had abolished the slave trade in its empire in 1807,

British soldiers filing into the Ethiopian hills followed the old trade route toward the Red Sea. (From *Illustrated London News*, July 4, 1868)

and Egypt later tried to do the same with British help. At first, the explorer Samuel Baker was assigned to end the slave trade, but he had little success. Then General Charles Gordon arrived, and the campaign began to succeed.

Gordon ruled as Governor-General of the province of Equatoria from his capital at Khartoum. (The British had taken over this part of Africa and renamed it "Equatoria.")

Gordon brought the area's ivory trade under government control. He drove the Arab traders out of the slave business. He even traveled up the Nile himself but wrote quite contemptuously of the country he found:

> A more dreary, weary set of marches you cannot conceive. The country is quite uninhabited—a vast undulating prairie of jungle grass and scrub-trees....Everything relating to this country has been much exaggerated.

Eventually, the Arab merchants were driven back, out of the upper Nile and into the Sudan, into Kordofan and Darfur.

THE MAHDI

A New Prophet. In 1881, a 37-year-old man named Muhammad Ahmad declared himself the long-awaited Mahdi. Muhammad Ahmad came from a family of former slave and ivory merchants who had been driven out of business by the British.

Muhammad Ahmad had begun to attract a following among the people of the upper Nile 20 years earlier as a highly respected *sufi*, or Moslem holy man. But he did not declare himself Mahdi until the summer of 1881. In 1881–1882, revolts in the Egyptian army led the British to occupy the lower Nile directly. That was when the Mahdi made his move in an attempt to drive the British out of Egypt.

First the Mahdi took El Obeid on the Sudan Route. He then defeated a British army sent to retake the surrounding province of Kordofan. After that, his rule spread to Darfur, to the western rivers that flowed from the Nile, and along the pilgrims' route through the Red Sea hills. General Gordon had returned to England, but he was called back to Khartoum to get the Egyptians and British out safely.

Canoes Along the Nile. Canadian *voyageurs*, or canoe travelers, were sent to help Gordon in 1884. The idea was that they could use their canoes to help evacuate people. But this part of the Nile was cataract, or waterfall, country. It was not easy to move upstream on such a river:

> The Nile boat…is from 30 to 32 feet long, 6 or 7 in beam. From 8 to 12 soldiers were told off [assigned] to each boat, and one voyageur….
>
> As a usual thing six men pulled. The voyageur took the rudder, sometimes the bow. When the boat came to a strong current, the men would pull their best, and with a good way on would get up, but if they failed and were carried back, I have seen them make the attempt a second and third time, straining every nerve, and then succeed. If it was impossible to row up, all the crew but the bowman and the man at the rudder would disembark, get out their tracking line, put it over their shoulders, and walk along the back, tracking the boat, until they reached smooth water again. When they came to a bad rapid, instead of having one crew on the rope, 3, 4, or 5 crews, according to the rush of water, would be put on. This was avoided as much as possible, as it took 5 times as long. When it became necessary to place 30 or 40 men on the line it was generally necessary also to unload the arms, and perhaps part of the load. Great care had to be exercised to see that there should not be any slack rope, so that on the Nile you would hear the words from morning until night, "Pull up the slack," "Haul away." When the men were on the line and when all was ready the word would be given, "Shove off." If there was too much slack rope, the current would catch the boat, running her out into the stream broadside on, and sometimes filling the boat. She would turn over, throwing the voyageurs into the water, unless they were smart enough to climb over one side as she went under at the other, and then cling to the bottom, until taken off.

The canoes and all the other efforts did not alleviate the crisis. The peoples of the Nubian Nile rose up under the leadership of the Mahdi and they killed Gordon, overcame Khartoum, and took back the Sudan for themselves.

The Defeat of the Mahdi's Movement. A few months later, the Mahdi died. His successors tried to maintain a Moslem state in the Sudan, but they succeeded for only a few more years. In 1898, a large British force moved up the Nile and crushed the Moslem troops.

Once in power, the British built a railroad in the Nile country. It ran south along the west bank of the Nile, then along the east bank through Aswan and Wadi Halfa. The railroad then went across the Nubian Desert and down the Nile again to Khartoum. Further extensions of the railroad followed the old caravan routes: through Sennar into Kenya and from Khartoum to Omdurman, El Obeid, and then west.

THE PERIOD OF EUROPEAN CONTROL

This was the period of the partition (division) of Africa. By the end of the 19th century, just about all of Africa had been conquered. The French ruled most of the Sahara and western Africa except for Nigeria. The British controlled the east, including Egypt and the eastern Sudan. The Portuguese, Dutch, and Germans controlled other parts of the continent.

Despite the death of the Mahdi, people continued to look to the east. Some made pilgrimages along the routes to the Red Sea on their way to Mecca. Many simply migrated.

Sometimes famines caused large numbers of people to leave their homes and move eastward since religious Moslems wanted to be near Mecca if they were going to die.

Many of these pilgrims did make it as far as Mecca. Others simply stopped along the upper Nile where they became part of a more prosperous Egyptian culture. Many industries, especially cotton, took advantage of this migrant labor, since these travelers could be paid lower wages than native Egyptians.

Many of the monuments shown here, on the banks of the Nile and on the Philae Islands in the river, were covered by the waters of the Aswan High Dam in the 1960s, though some were preserved. (From L.W. Yaggy and T.L. Haines, *Museum of Antiquity*, 1882)

Railroads in the Sudan followed the old trade routes. They came to form the boundaries between the nations of modern Africa: Chad was formed in the central Sudan; Ethiopia was founded in the east; and smaller countries were formed along the Red Sea.

Modern Times

The Nile itself was divided along its natural boundary lines. When the British finally left the area after World War II, the border between Egypt and the Sudan was drawn just north of the Second Cataract.

This area is also the site of the great Aswan dam. The old dam of 1906 was replaced by a huge new one during the 1960s. It created the huge Lake Nasser, which also extends across the border into Sudan.

Trade and travel are very different in Egypt now from what they were centuries ago. But the older caravan routes—sometimes replaced by automobile highways, sometimes in their original form—still follow the line of the Nile as it cuts into the heart of Africa.

Suggestions for Further Reading

Arkell, A. J. *A History of the Sudan: From the Earliest Times to 1821. Second Edition* (London: University of London, the Athlone Press, 1961). A valuable review with an archaeological emphasis.

Baines, John, and Jaromir Malek. *Atlas of Ancient Egypt* (New York: Facts On File, 1980). A beautifully illustrated study of the Egyptian sites.

Ibn Battuta. *Travels A.D. 1325–1354*, in three volumes (Cambridge: University Press, 1958–71). Hakluyt Society Publications, Second Series. Translated by H. A. R. Gibb. A fine edition with helpful maps.

Bruce, James. *Travels to Discover the Source of the Nile* (New York: Horizon Press, 1964). Selected and edited by C. F. Beckingham. An abridgment of the 1804 Second Edition; first published in 1790.

Fairservis, Walter A., Jr. *The Ancient Kingdoms of the Nile and the Doomed Monuments of Nubia* (New York: Thomas Y. Crowell,

1962). An overview, incorporating quotations from modern travelers.

Jarvis, H. Wood. *Pharaoh to Farouk* (New York: Macmillan, 1955). A popular history focusing on the modern period.

July, Robert W. *A History of the African People*, second edition (New York: Scribner's, 1974). A useful general history.

Ludwig, Emil. *The Nile: The Life-Story of a River* (New York: Viking, 1937). Translated by Mary H. Lindsay. A popular and personal work.

Moorehead, Alan. *The Blue Nile* (New York: Harper & Row, 1962). Western explorations from 1798 through the 19th century.

———. *The White Nile* (New York: Harper & Row, 1960). Western explorations from the 1850's to 1900.

Al-Naqur, 'Umar. *The Pilgrimage Tradition in West Africa: An Historical Study with Special Reference to the Nineteenth Century* (Khartoum: Khartoum University Press, 1972). A specialist work drawing on many firsthand accounts.

3

THE INCENSE ROAD AND THE PILGRIMAGE ROAD: EARLY HISTORY

A SACRED ROAD IN THREE RELIGIONS

> And when the queen of Sheba heard of the fame of Solomon...she came to Jerusalem with a very great train, with camels that bare [carried] spices, and very much gold, and precious stones...And she gave the king an hundred and twenty talents of gold, and of spices very great store, and precious stones; there came no more such abundance of spices as these which the queen of Sheba gave to king Solomon.

In this passage from the Old Testament of the Bible, the Queen of Sheba probably followed the Incense Road, an ancient trade route. The Incense Road was used for thousands of years to carry spices and other goods up through Arabia to the great kingdoms along the Mediterranean Sea, such as Egypt and Israel.

Besides being a trade route, the Incense Road was important in three religions—Judaism, Christianity, and Islam. Abraham, the father of the Jewish religion, followed part of the Incense Road when he led his people to the new land of Canaan, an area now known as Jordan and Israel.

Jesus, the central figure of the Christian religion, received gifts at his birth that had come along the old Incense Road. Later, Jesus' disciple Paul used the Incense Road to spread the message of Christianity. Finally, Moslems, the followers of the Islam religion, used the Incense Road to make religious journeys, or pilgrimages, to Mecca, their holy city. Because of this, the Incense Road later came to be known as the Pilgrimage Road.

Where the Road Went

The Incense Road ran from the Hadramaut, the southern coastal strip of the Arabian Peninsula, to Yemen, in the southwest corner of Arabia. Then it ran up the east coast of Arabia (today's country of Saudi Arabia), along the Red Sea, until it reached the land of Jordan.

From the city of Amman, Jordan, one branch of the Incense Road continued north through the ancient city of Damascus (in today's Syria). There the Incense Road intersected with another great trade route—the Great Desert Route. Another branch of the Incense Road broke off in Jordan to go west, across the Sinai Desert, into the land of Egypt.

The exact route of the Incense Road varied over the centuries as different cities rose in prominence at different times. Trade routes always vary their exact paths to accommodate cities that have become large trading centers.

Early Days of the Incense Road

Nomads and Herders. No exact date for the beginning of the Incense Road is known. The first trade along the route probably started with the travels of the *nomadic*, or wandering desert Arabs. These nomads moved their herds according to the season. When the Arabian Desert started to become very dry in the spring they drove the herds north into the Syrian Desert. There was more water in the Syrian Desert, so it was a better place to spend the summer.

At some point, these nomads probably began loading their animals with goods to trade along the way. Thus the first trade in the region began.

Abraham's Journey. From the north, herders and traders of ancient times moved in an arc from Mesopotamia (an ancient kingdom located in today's country of Iraq) into Syria and Palestine (today's countries of Israel and Jordan). This arc was the route followed by Abraham shortly after 2000 B.C. Abraham is described

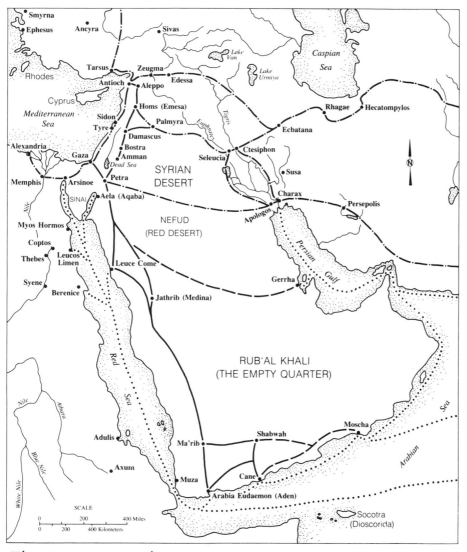

The Incense Road in Greco-Roman Times

——— Main Incense Road   —·—·— Main Connecting Land Routes
– – – Secondary Incense Roads ········Spice Route

in the Old Testament of the Bible as the founder of Judaism. According to Jewish teaching, Abraham heard a command from God to "go forth unto a land that I will show thee."

Abraham's belief in one God spread all along the route he took. It even spread down the Incense Road into Arabia, as traders and travelers talked about Abraham's beliefs.

For thousands of years, frankincense was harvested from trees like these in southern Arabia. (Engraving from Thevet, *Cosmographia Universelle*, 1575, reprinted in *Bible Educator*)

Scented Products of the Incense Road. The region covered by the Incense Road was warmer and moister than it is today, and the low-lying southern coast, especially the main valley of the Hadramaut, fostered disease. As late as the 1st century A.D., an anonymous Greek mariner described these diseases in his guidebook, *Periplus of the Erythraean [Red] Sea*:

The country is unhealthy in the extreme, pestilential even to those who sail along the coast, and mortal to the wretched sufferers employed in collecting the frankincense, who perish likewise as often by want (and neglect) as by the pernicious influence of the climate. The country inland is mountainous and difficult in access; the air is foggy, and loaded with vapors caused (it is supposed) by the noxious exhalations from the trees that bear the incense.

Others thought these incense trees smelled very good. In the 2nd century B.C., the writer Agatharchides, from Alexandria, Egypt, thought the Hadramaut coast was quite attractive:

A heavenly and indescribable fragrance seems to strike and stir the senses of everyone. Even far out from the land as you sail past you do not miss a share in this enjoyment. For in the spring, whenever a wind arises from the land, it happens that the fragrant odors blowing from the myrrh bushes and others of the kind reach the neighboring parts of the sea.

The scented products from southern Arabia were frankincense, balsam, and myrrh, which were harvested from local trees. These perfumes were used principally in religious ceremonies.

The Growth of Trade. We do not know when Arabia began serious trading along the Incense Road. We do know that Arabians tamed the one-humped camel by around 1800 B.C. The taming of the camel was an important step in trade, for camels could travel long distances in the hot, dry desert. Once camels could be used to carry goods, it was possible for traders to travel farther and faster.

In southern Arabia, the Incense Road connected with the trade routes of the sailors from India who brought spices, silks, and jewels from the Far East. By 2000 B.C., Egypt was already receiving supplies of cinnamon brought by these Indian sailors. The Egyptians used cinnamon in *embalming*, or preserving, dead bodies.

The sailors from the east were not able to make use of the Red Sea to bring their goods directly into Egypt since it had contrary winds, dangerous reefs, and many pirates. So they began to bring their goods to the harbor of Arabia Eudaemon (today's city of Aden in the People's Democratic Republic of Yemen).

In Arabia Eudaemon, the sailors sold their goods to Arab traders who would take the spices and jewels north by camel caravans. (A caravan is a large group of people and animals that travels through dangerous or desert regions.) These caravans carried goods up the Incense Road to the countries of the Mediterranean.

By the time of Solomon, in the late 10th century B.C., these southern caravans were mainly in the hands of the Sabaean, or Sheban, people. Many people now believe that the Queen of Sheba's famous visit to Solomon was because the queen wanted to hold on to her monopoly of the spice trade.

Arab Prosperity. At this time, the Arabians were a prosperous people. In the thousand years before the birth of Christ, almost every description of the Arabians mentions their prosperity. Writing around the time of Christ, the Greek geographer Strabo agreed. He mentioned especially the tribes of the Gerrhaeans and the Sabaeans, whom he said were

> the richest of all the tribes, and possess a great quantity of wrought articles in gold and silver, as couches, tripods, basins, drinking vessels, to which we must add the costly magnificence of their houses; for the doors, walls, and roofs are variegated with inlaid ivory, gold, silver and precious stones.

Strabo also wrote about the Incense Road itself:

> Those tribes who live close to one another receive in continuous succession the load of aromatics [sweet-smelling perfumes] and deliver them to their next neighbors as far as Syria and Mesopotamia.

In other words, trade took place as the precious goods were passed from tribe to tribe along the road.

SHABWAH, MA'RIB, AND PETRA

Ancient Cities. Trade on the Incense Road led to a number of cities on that route becoming rich and prosperous. The main city on the souther end of the Incense Road was Shabwah. Today, Shabwah has been swallowed up by the desert. So have many of its neighbors. But traces of the old route and even a few portions of paved road can still be seen.

Some parts of the Incense Road have narrow passages built into them. Scholars think this might have been in order to force caravans to pass through single file, one person at a time. That way, each person could be forced to pay taxes on the goods he or she carried or to pay a toll, or a charge, for using the road. Any government able to force people to pay taxes and tolls could make a profit from the trade that took place.

Another ancient city along the Incense Road was Ma'rib. It was the capital of Saba. In ancient days, Ma'rib was known for its huge

dam. People used the dam to store water for drinking and for their crops.

Petra, a thriving city just east of the Sinai Desert, was a third city where many caravans stopped. From Petra, the Incense Road forked into two branches—one to Egypt, the other to Syria. This ancient city was known for its beauty since many of its buildings were built with rose-red stone.

At several places along the Incense Road, Arabians had cut passes through the mountain rock. In some places, they even had cut stairs. At Petra, however, they carved an entire city out of the side of a mountain. Petra is built inside a crater faced with sheer cliffs. The early Arabians cut many homes and, later, thousands of tombs into these cliffs.

Other ancient cities have long since been buried under sand. But Petra remains standing for all to see. In his book Caravan Cities, Michael Rostovtzeff describes visiting Petra in the 1930s. He imagines what it was like when Petra was the prime city on the Incense Road:

> [Here] bargains were concluded, here bankers, merchants, middle-men, and their agents carried on their business, here gold and

The trading city of Petra—with its tombs cut out of cliffs—was set in a rocky gorge entered by narrow, easily defended passes through the barren hills. ("Eastern End of the Valley," from David Roberts, *The Holy Land*, 1829) precious stones changed hands, here ginger peel and thyme smelt sweetly and the air was filled with the pleasant perfume of incense and that of other odorous leaves and roots brought from India and Arabia.

Far-Reaching Trade. From Petra, trade on the Syrian branch of the Incense Road went north through Amman, Damascus, and Emesa (today's city of Hams) to the crossroads of Aleppo.

In Aleppo, the Incense Road joined with two other great trade routes: the Great Desert Route which went through Mesopotamia, and the Silk Road which went thousands of miles east, all the way to China.

ROMAN TIMES

The Roman Empire. Prosperity was a magnet that drew many peoples to the Incense Road. Many tried to take control of the Road's rich trade, and some even succeeded for a time. For the most part, however, no one group could control the Incense Road. Then the Romans came.

Roman movement into the Middle East shaped events in that region. When the Romans first came to the area, they tried to trade with the East without going through the Arabs as middlemen. They hired Greek sailors and opened up full-scale trading on the Red Sea. They thought that if they sailed directly to India themselves, they would not have to depend on Arab caravans to bring goods from southern Arabia.

The Roman army also tried to conquer the Arabs, but they were not equipped to fight the local people in a land unknown to them. According to the Greek geographer Strabo, Arabian "merchants on camels with many people and animals can make their way safely and unimpeded amongst the hills and rocks, so that they have no need to fear even an army."

After six months, the Roman army left. The Arabs were used to traveling in the desert—but it was too much for the Romans. Since the Romans couldn't defeat the Arabs, they decided to trade with them. What they couldn't achieve in war they ended up achieving in business. Eventually, the Romans took control of the whole Mediterranean section of the Incense Road, down through the region of Petra. This area became the Roman province of Arabia Petraea.

Roman Roads. Everywhere the Romans conquered new lands, they built roads. These roads were used to transport armies of Roman soldiers that kept control of Roman territory. Roman government officials also traveled on these roads or sent messages by them. Once the roads were completed, they were also used as obvious trading routes. Arabia Petraea was no exception. The Romans built roads throughout the region. Sometimes they used old tracks. Other times they built new roads.

In the desert regions, the Romans sank wells at least every 28 miles. That way, a traveler was never more than a day's trip away from water. The Romans also erected forts for their soldiers and border guards.

The Romans also constructed *caravanserais* that made caravan trading easier. Caravanserais were places where caravans could stop and were built just inside city gates. Here weary merchants would find shops to supply their needs, storerooms for their goods, marketplaces where they could sell their wares, and rooms where they could stay while they were in the city. The Romans also built graveyards, or necropolises, into the cities' surrounding cliffs.

Khans or caravanserais like this one at Damascus gave shelter to traveling merchants and pilgrims for many centuries. (From Douglas Carruthers, *The Desert Route to India*)

Trade on the Incense Road. The city of Petra received goods both from the southern part of the Incense Road and from the Red Sea port of Aela. Before the Romans came, Petra had also received goods from the Persian Gulf. These goods usually went to Mesopotamia, but because of fighting there, sometimes they were detoured to Petra. To reach Petra, caravans had to follow difficult desert routes across the Arabian peninsula.

When the Romans came, they made the whole region safer and more peaceful. Ironically, this led to hard times for Petra. In peaceful times, caravans did not need to detour through Petra. Instead, they went straight to Bostra.

On the southern part of the Incense Road, the Sabaeans gradually gave way to a new power, the Himyarites. This new power still used the city of Ma'rib as its capital. The Himyarites were not sailors. They gradually dropped out of sea trading. Thus they became dependent on others to bring them goods for trade on the Incense Road.

AFTER ROME

The Roman Empire was a powerful force for many centuries. But eventually, its power began to decline. As the Roman Empire declined, its huge markets shrank. Generally, trade declined because Roman soldiers no longer protected travelers and because Roman roads and trade routes were no longer kept in good repair.

Thus the Incense Road fell on harder times. Arabia was so weakened that Yemen was conquered two times by the kingdom of Axum (part of today's country of Ethiopia) from across the Red Sea. Once in the 4th century A.D. and again in the 6th century, the Axumites conquered the Yemenites.

The people of Axum were Christians of mixed Arab and African heritage. They never fully controlled Yemen. But Arabia's attempts to throw them out upset travel along the Incense Road.

When the Axumites were finally forced to leave, the Persians, ancestors of today's Iranians, moved down into Yemen. Cities on the Incense Road suffered. The old southern capital of Ma'rib was abandoned. The new capital, San'a, was more protected from coastal attack. It was also better supplied with water, which was important, as the region's climate had become dryer by this time.

Mecca. We don't know the date when the Incense Road began to pass through Mecca. But by the 6th century A.D., it was already a large trade center and place of pilgrimage.

Like Petra and many other cities on the route, Mecca was set in a gorge in inland mountains. Geographer R. Blanchard describes the place as "unbelievably bare, rocky crags with no scrap of soil, sharp, jagged, broken edges, sheer from top to bottom."

The gorge of Mecca was so narrow that the infrequent, violent rainstorms of the region could flood it. There was one important shrine, the Ka'bah, in Mecca that many pilgrims went to see on their religious journey. If the gorge was flooded, pilgrims sometimes had to swim to the shrine. This still happens occasionally, even in modern times.

The Birth of Mohammed. In this place, Mohammed—the founder of the religion of Islam—was born in about A.D. 570. Mohammed's life changed the history of the region.

Mohammed's ties with the Incense Road were very close. Before he was even born, his father died on the way back to Mecca, returning from the trading port of Gaza. By the time Mohammed was six, his mother had also died. He was now a poor relation, cared for only by a rich merchant uncle. According to an old legend, this uncle took young Mohammed with him on a trip up the Incense Road to Syria. Arabic writer Tabari writes of what is supposed to have happened on this trip:

> When the company halted at Bostra in Syria, there was a monk named Bahira, who dwelt in a hermitage there and who was well-read in the learning of the Christians....This year, when the caravan halted near Bahira, he prepared much food for them. While he was in his hermitage, he had seen the Envoy of Allah [that is, the messenger of God] among his companions; and a cloud covered him with its shadow....he questioned the Envoy of Allah about the things he felt when he was awake or asleep....Then he exam-ined...[Mohammed's] back and found the seal of prophecy between his shoulders.

According to this story, Mohammed was thus marked for great-ness from an early age. Some scholars question whether or not this trip actually took place. But the story does show the significance of the Incense Road to the Moslems.

Mohammed Becomes a Trader.   During his early years, Mohammed often found shelter and support among both Jews and Christians. Indeed, the doctor charged with protecting his life was a Jew. While still poor, Mohammed educated himself in many ways. One way was to listen to "legends about the ancients" told by religious refugees—Jews and Christians.

Then a rich widow, 15 years older, let the 23-year-old Mohammed lead her caravan to Syria. There he bought Byzantine goods to sell in the Mecca market. Mohammed married this woman and remained a rich trader for some years.

In A.D. 610, while meditating in a cave outside Mecca, near the end of the Arab month of Ramadan, Mohammed received his first call from God. According to the Moslem religion, this call commanded him to bring to his people a new religion and a sacred book. The sacred book of this new religion was called the Koran.

The Growth of Islam.   Some of Mohammed's family were early converts to the Islamic religion. But most of his family resisted Mohammed—for they were making money from the pilgrims of a more established religion visiting a sacred shrine in Mecca. If people took up a new religion, Mohammed's family would no longer profit from these pilgrims.

Then, in 622, Mohammed and his followers made their famous Hegira (migration) along the Incense Road to the city of Jathrib. As a result, the city was renamed Medina, or al-Madinah, the City of the Prophet. (Medina is in today's country of Saudi Arabia.)

Mohammed's followers were increasing, and in 624, in the month of Ramadan, Mohammed decided to attack a caravan bound for Mecca south of Medina. Mohammed had only 300 Moslems, but they defeated the 1,000 Moroccans who came to the aid of the caravan. From then on, Mohammed's victories drew more and more converts to his new religion.

The Development of the Religion.   Mohammed gained Moslems the right to visit Mecca in 628. By 630 he was so strong that he and his followers took over the city. He himself destroyed the idols in the ancient shrine there.

Medina continued to be Mohammed's capital. But Mecca became his religious center, and Mohammed decreed as part of the religion of Islam that all Moslems had to make at least one pilgrimage, or religious journey, to Mecca, sometime during their lifetime. And only faithful Moslems were to be allowed into Mecca.

In the same year, 630, Mohammed took his religion north into Syria. Then, in 632, Mohammed died. For a short time, this stopped the spread of Islam along the Incense Road.

Mecca: The Holy City. Mecca was the center of the small but strong Islamic world. So other regions were named with reference to it. The area around Mecca was called the Hejaz. The northern, Syrian part of the Incense Road was called esh-Shem, which meant that it was on the left hand of those who faced Mecca from the west. The southern part of Arabia, once called Arabia Eudaemon, was now called Yemen, which meant that it was on the right hand of Mecca.

After Mohammed's death, Moslems expanded their influence north, east, and west. In only a dozen years, they conquered the territory around the Incense Road north past Aleppo. In little more than a century, they had built an empire to rival Rome's. In Chapter 4, we will look at the rise of this Islam world along the Incense Road.

4

THE INCENSE ROAD
AND THE
PILGRIMAGE ROAD:
LATER HISTORY

THE CARAVANS

Pilgrimage Caravans In the early days of Islam, in the seventh century A.D., the caravans to Mecca headed north each winter. These caravans consisted of religious Moslems making their required pilgrimages. They traveled by caravan because the journey was too difficult and dangerous to make alone. They chose winter for the trip because that was the season when there was the most water and pasture available for their animals.

These early caravans needed many animals, for the travelers rode on animals and used animals to carry their supplies. These caravans often included 2,500 to 3,000 camels and 100 to 300 guards along with many merchants, camel drivers, servants, and overseers (the people who told the servants what to do and punished them if they did not obey).

The Bashis—Leaders of the Caravan. The early caravans had a very well-designed system of organization. The leader of the caravan was called the *bashi*. The bashi, who was always a male, was fully responsible for the caravan. This was a huge responsibility because almost everyone who lived in Mecca had some money

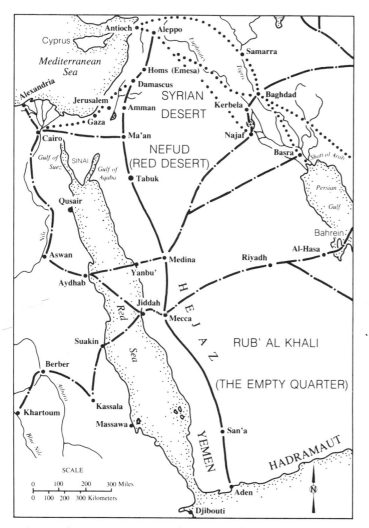

The Pilgrimage Road in Modern Times
———— Darb el-Hajj
— · — · — Other Main Routes to Mecca
· · · · · · · · Main Connecting Land Routes

invested in it. A Mecca resident may have given some caravan trader money to buy goods or may have sold animals or supplies to someone with the caravan.

Thus the entire welfare of the city depended on the bashi's good judgment. If the caravan lost any money, the bashi was responsible for compensation.

The bashis led the caravans personally. They chose the exact route. If they thought the caravan needed extra protection against ambushes by local thieves, it was up to them to hire more guards in the local towns along the way. The bashis were responsible for maintaining good relations with the nomads along the route. These nomads were wanderers who drove their herds through the desert, always looking for water and pasture to feed their own animals. Sometimes nomads attacked a caravan, and it was up to the bashis to keep this from happening.

Moslem pilgrims would sometimes gather in Yemen, where they might be guarded on their way by soldiers like these. (From N. Niebuhr, *Description de l'Arabie*, Copenhagen)

The bashis also kept discipline within the caravan. They made sure that people did not fight or argue and that they did not do anything that would endanger the lives of others.

The Daleels—Pilots of the Caravan. An assistant to the bashi was the daleel, or pilot. The pilot was also always male. The job of piloting was passed down within families. Many pilots had learned their skills from their fathers or uncles. The daleel handled many of the details of the caravan's progress, such as how long to march, when to stop, and the exact path to take. The decision of just where and when to camp depended partly on the region's local nomads. Some nomads were robbers, which meant that extra guards were needed when the caravan stopped for the night. Other nomads welcomed the arrival of the caravan and turned the occasion into a fair.

Caravan Messengers. The caravans also employed many different types of messengers. When messengers were sent with bad news, they were called *nadeers*. Nadeers wore torn clothes and rode on backwards saddles. That way, townspeople could see from a long way off that the messenger was carrying bad news and could send help quickly. When messengers had good news, they were called *basheers*. When the basheers arrived the townspeople would begin beating drums to announce the coming of the caravan and the beginning of that year's fair.

THE PILGRIMAGE ROAD

Moslem Pilgrims. The spread of Islam brought pilgrims to the Incense Road in great numbers. Pilgrims had been journeying to Mecca for centuries, but now the Koran, the Moslems' holy book, said that the pilgrimage was a service to Allah (the Moslem word for God). So every year, thousands of people made the pilgrimage.

The final destination of the pilgrimage to Mecca was the Ka'bah, a cubelike structure that houses the Black Stone. According to Moslem beliefs, the Black Stone was given to Adam when he was thrown out of Paradise. The Black Stone was supposed to help Adam gain forgiveness for his sins of disobeying God. Faithful Moslems were required to wear special dress as they walked around the Ka'bah and then the stone. Most pilgrims also visited Mohammed's tomb in nearby Medina as part of their pilgrimage.

In the late seventh century, the Umayyad Caliphs (Islamic spiritual rulers) in the area that today is called Syria designated the ancient city of Damascus as their capital. Pilgrims began to gather there each year to form a religious caravan to Mecca. The Incense Road then came to be known as the Darb el-Hajj, or the Pilgrimage Road.

Splits Within Islam. The Moslems were far from united. After Mohammed's death, there were many arguments about who was to lead Islam. This led to a split that still exists today: the majority group consists of the Sunni Moslems and the smaller group consists of the the Shiites, or Shia Moslems.

The Sunnis were led by the Umayyad Caliphs of Damascus. The Shiites, however, split away from their leadership in the middle of the 8th century to set up their own rulers, the Abbasids. The Abbasids were based in Baghdad in the modern country of Iraq.

No matter to which group a Moslem belonged, however, they all agreed on the importance of the pilgrimage. Sometimes the Sunnis and the Shiites were at war. But most of the time they were able to share the same pilgrimage caravans—even if there was tension.

Changes in the Route. As Islam spread in all directions, pilgrims began to gather at other points for their journey. Eventually, however, all of the routes fed into the Pilgrimage Road.

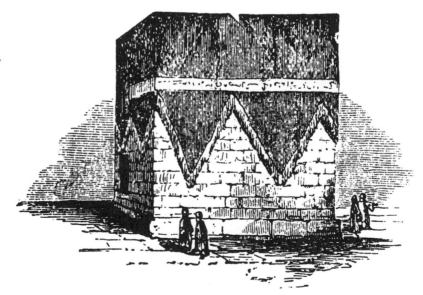

At the center of the mosque at Mecca was the cube-shaped covered stone shrine, called the *Ka'bah*, which housed the sacred Black Stone. (From Richard F. Burton, *Personal Narrative of a Pilgrimage to Al-Madinah & Mecca*, Vol. II, 1893 ed.)

Many Moslem romances featured a pilgrimage to Mecca and the Ka'bah. (From Niza, *Khamseh*, 1442, MS. Add. 25900 f. 114v, British Library)

This road itself varied over the centuries. It was hardly a major highway at any time, even with the heavy pilgrimage traffic and the continuing trade caravans. Indeed, it barely stood out from its desert surroundings, even after centuries of use.

The modern historian Christina Grant noted that much of the Incense/Pilgrimage Road was simply empty desert with only a single beaten path to show where caravans had been forced into a narrow route over many centuries of travel. Elsewhere, the route was marked by the "bleached bones and the skeletons of camels, horses, and mules," and the "little mounds of rock" that marked the graves of pilgrims who had died on the way to Mecca.

Hardships of the Trip. Such deaths were not uncommon. Sick people were not required to make the trip to Mecca, but the 900-mile trip was hard even for healthy travelers. This long trip, from Damascus to Mecca, had to be made in 40 days and 40 nights.

No one is sure why this 40-day limit was imposed. Some people believe that the camel-owners and contractors insisted on this time, because they wanted to increase their own profits and felt that the cost of feeding the animals and supplying food to their guards would be too high if the trip lasted much longer. Other people think that because of the general lack of water in the desert, it was important to make the trip quickly before the caravans' own water supplies ran out. As it was, much of the traveling had to take place in the cool night, out of the day's heat.

Government Help to the Pilgrims. The pilgrims did not always have to prepare for and pay the costs of the *hajj* (pilgrimage) by themselves. Some governments supported the hajj from the early days of Islam. Moslem rulers often provided water and fortified shelter along the way.

In especially dry areas, the rulers dug reservoirs so travelers would always find water along the way. These reservoirs were filled by canals from a nearby oasis or by water-carriers who hauled in water from further away in time for the caravan's arrival. A government hajj fund paid for the water-carriers and for soldiers to staff forts. The hajj fund also paid for the cost of shipping supplies to the forts so pilgrims could buy supplies along the way.

Rich Moslems who could not make the hajj themselves often helped other pilgrims financially. Moslem women were not allowed to make the trip without escorts. If they could not make the trip, they too often helped others.

Trading in the Caravans. The pilgrimage was not only used for religious purposes, it was also used for trade. Merchants often joined the caravans to sell their wares to the pilgrims or along the way.

Many pilgrims combined business and religion, and merchants were often given special protection by the religious travelers. The

Roman traveler Ludovicus Vertomannus accompanied a 16th-century pilgrimage caravan. He noted that when they were under attack, the camels were used as a wall. The merchants were placed . in the center of the protected area "while the pilgrims fought manfully on every side."

THE MOSLEM POSTAL SYSTEM

Government Messengers. These caravan roads served government purposes as well. A hajj caravan was like a traveling city of thousands of people. It took 40 days to go from Damascus to Mecca. But a fast-moving courier (messenger) might make the trip in only a few days. So the Umayyad Caliphs set up a regular postal service with riders moving along the Pilgrimage Road. These couriers, which the Moslems called *berids*, were government messengers.

The berids carried reports from the provinces to the Caliphs' capital. They took messages twice a week in normal times and more often in emergencies. Sometimes they collected taxes for the government. If individuals had a special permit, the couriers could also carry private messages for them.

Couriers wore a silver plaque around their necks identifying them as the Sultan's (ruler's) messengers. They also wore yellow scarves on their backs. These scarves identified them as eligible to get fresh horses at the relay stations along the road. This enabled them to keep on riding at top speed. Couriers on the Cairo-Damascus road generally completed the journey in four days. The trip to or from Aleppo took one day more.

Post stations, called *khans* or *caravanserais*, were built along the route in the countryside or in towns. They provided fresh horses, water, food, and modest shelter for the couriers. They made travel on the Incense Road even easier and safer than it had been before.

The Ottoman Turks. In the 15th century, the Mongols invaded the Middle East. The Mongols rode into Syria from the country that we know today as Mongolia. This invasion disrupted the courier system and all other travel on the Pilgrimage Road.

Then, in the middle of the 16th century, the Ottoman Turks took control of the Middle East. The Turks set up a different type of courier system that offered one group of couriers for local service and another group for long-distance service to their capital, Constantinople. The Ottoman government also had special dispatch-bearers called *tatars* who carried important messages or precious commodities such as gold.

Large cities like Aleppo had their own courier systems. These were all under the control of the local sheik, or ruler, who set the service charges. The amount charged depended on the season, the danger, and the speed desired.

Carrier Pigeons and Cannons. Carrier pigeons formed another system of communication along the old Incense Road. The pigeons flew in relays from specially built towers about 50 miles apart. Flying in relays meant that each pigeon only went 50 miles on the journey, from one tower to the next. At each tower, people took the message from the arriving pigeon and tied it to a fresh one, which they then sent on its way. These pigeon relays could sometimes complete in only a few hours a delivery that would have taken people several days.

A special courier system was used by the pilgrimage caravan. When the caravan left Damascus, a team of five couriers went with it. Then, at the cities of Ma'an, Mada'in, Medina, Mina, and Tabuk, a courier would speed for home with letters from the pilgrims. This mail was so important to the friends and relatives waiting at home that when the couriers arrived with it, a cannon was fired three times from the Damascus fort to signal its arrival.

THE CAIRO CARAVANS

In the early centuries, Damascus and Baghdad were the main centers where pilgrims gathered to make their journeys to Mecca. Later, Cairo became the political capital of the Moslem world, and pilgrims from all the other cities would gather first in Cairo.

Each major city would send a caravan to Cairo headed by a *mahmil*, a specially decorated, throne-like litter, or tent, mounted on a camel. Cairo's mahmil, which first appeared during a holiday that started the pilgrimage season, then led the whole caravan to Mecca.

Many pilgrims and traders traveled to Cairo and the Pilgrimage Road by crossing the Sinai Desert. This desert route was well supplied with shelter. But merchants and traders who crossed the desert had to be prepared to pay taxes to the governments and to show passports as they crossed between Egypt and Syria.

Here is a description by the great 14th-century Arab traveler, Ibn Battuta:

Without its elaborate covering, the *mahmil* was just a simple frame of wood, mounted on the back of a camel. (From Richard F. Burton, *Personal Narrative of a Pilgrimage to Al-Madinah & Mecca*, Vol. I, 1893 ed.)

At each of these stations [shelters] there is a hostelry [hotel], which they call a *khan*, where travelers alight with their beasts, and outside each *khan* is a public watering-place and a shop at which the traveler may buy what he requires for himself and his beast. Amongst these stations is the well-known place called Qatya...where *zakat* (an alms tax) is collected from the merchants, their goods are examined, and their baggage most rigorously searched. There are government offices here, with officers, clerks, and notaries, and its daily revenue is a thousand gold dinars. No one may pass this place in the direction of Syria without passport from Egypt, nor into Egypt without a passport from Syria, as a measure of protection for a person's property and of precaution against spies from Iraq. This road is under guarantee of the bedouins (that is to say, they have been made responsible for guarding it) [the bedouins were local Arabs]. At nightfall they smooth down the sand so that no mark is left on it, then the governor comes in the morning and examines the sand. If he finds any track on it he requires the Arabs to fetch the person who made it, and they set out in pursuit of him and never fail to catch him. They then bring him to the governor, who punishes him as he sees fit.

As pilgrims approached Mecca, whether by land or sea, they were told to put on the Moslem's special religious clothes, the *ihram*. The men shaved their heads, cut their nails, trimmed their mustaches, and bathed themselves. Then they dressed in two large cloths, one wrapped around the waist and extending to the ankles, the other draped over one shoulder and tied at the waist. Their heads and insteps (the arched part of the foot) were kept completely bare.

Women pilgrims covered themselves from head to foot in white garments. Instead of the normal veil that religious Moslem women wore over the lower halves of their faces, they put on palm-leaf masks. This mask totally covered the face, leaving only two eye-holes. Special pilots then guided the women through the last parts of the pilgrimage.

Pilgrims approaching Mecca had to put on special clothes like these, the woman being completely covered, except the two eye-holes in her palm-leaf mask. (From Richard F. Burton, *Personal Narrative of a Pilgrimage to Al-Madinah & Mecca*, Vol. II, 1893 ed.)

European Explorers. In the 15th and 16th centuries, European explorers began visiting the countries of the Middle East. They were mainly interested in forging a connection with the valuable Spice Route, a network of sea lanes that brought spices, silks, and jewels from China and the Far East to the Middle East. From the Middle East, these goods had been taken across the Mediterranean by Arab middlemen where they were then traded to Europe.

In addition to their commercial interest in the region, Europeans were curious about Middle Eastern culture, especially about the fabled cities they had heard of that were supposed to be made of gold. Gradually, a few Europeans began to appear on the Pilgrimage Road.

An Italian's Journey. In 1503, the Italian Ludovicus Vertomannus joined the Damascus caravan to Mecca. He estimated this huge group to include 40,000 men and 35,000 camels with an escort of 60 Mamelukes (Egyptian soldiers—see Chapters 1 and 2). Because non-Moslems were not allowed on this journey, Vertomannus went in disguise.

Vertomannus reported that the caravan had to fight off attackers more than once. In addition, the caravan itself was not very peaceful. But perhaps it was not surprising that there were occasionally some arguments, for Vertomannus found a remarkable mix of people on the journey:

> Here we found a marvelous number of strangers and peregrines, or pilgrims; of the which some came from Syria, some from Persia [modern-day Iran], and others from...the East Indies....I never saw in any place greater abundance and frequentation of peoples.

An Englishman's Journey. Another European who got a rare insider's view of a pilgrimage was Joseph Pitts. He was a young British sailor who was captured by Algerian pirates and forced to convert to Islam. He was taken on a pilgrimage in 1680.

Pitts reported that the main attraction in Mecca was the Beit Allah—the House of God, or temple. Inside the Beit Allah was the Ka'bah, and inside the Ka'bah was the Black Stone. Pitts described the ritual that pilgrims followed at the Beit Allah:

> At one corner of the Beat [Beit], there is a black stone fastened and framed in with silver plate [in later centuries, this was gold], and

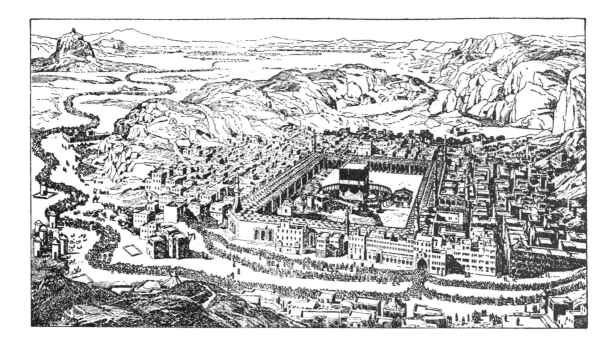

every time they come to that corner, they kiss the stone; and having gone round seven times they perform two...prayers.

This place is so much frequented by people going round it, that the place of the *Towoaf, i.e.* the circuit which they take in going round it, is seldom void of people at any time of the day or night. Many have waited several weeks, nay months, for the opportunity of finding it so.

The crowds were so thick that not everyone was able to kiss the stone, as Pitts noted:

In so great a resort as this, it is not to be supposed that every individual can come to kiss the stone afore-mentioned; therefore, in such a case, the lifting up the hands towards it, smoothing down their faces and using a short expression of devotion...and so passing by it till opportunity of kissing it offers, is thought sufficient.

After other religious ceremonies, pilgrims were then led into the nearby mountains to visit El Arafat, the Mountain of Knowledge. Pitts reported: "There, they say, Adam first found and knew his wife Eve." Eve was said to be buried at the city of Jidda (in modern Saudi Arabia).

Later, the pilgrims went to another hill, called Mina, or Muna, where Abraham was said to have offered his son for sacrifice. In Jewish and Christian tradition, the son Abraham almost sacrificed was Isaac. In Moslem tradition, that son was Ishmael. In any case, the pilgrims pitched a tent city at this hill, throwing stones at certain pillars to defy the devil. They also offered sacrifices. Pitts reported:

> After they have thrown the seven stones on the first day (the country people having brought great flocks of sheep to be sold), every one buys a sheep and sacrifices it; some of which they give to their friends, some to the poor which come out of Mecca and the country adjacent, very ragged poor, and the rest they eat themselves.

That was the end of the pilgrimage. The pilgrims then put their ordinary clothes back on and began a great feast. In Pitts' time, there was "rejoicing with abundance of illuminations all night, shooting of guns, and fireworks flying in the air; for they reckon that all their sins are now done away, and they shall, when they die, go directly to heaven."

After the feast, the pilgrims headed for home. Some went directly back. Others made a stop at Medina, where Mohammed was buried. Pitts described the caravan's return.

> Having hired camels…[from] the carriers, we set out…if it happen that the camel dies by the way, the carrier is to supply us with

Pilgrims approached the city of Medina from a ridge to the west of the town, which lay on a desert plain. (From Richard F. Burton, *Personal Narrative of a Pilgrimage to Al-Madinah & Mecca*, Vol. I, 1893 ed.)

another; therefore, those carriers who come from Egypt to Mecca with the Caravan, bring with them several spare camels; for there is hardly a night passeth but many die upon the road....

The first day we set out from Mecca, it was without any order at all, all hurly burly; but the next day every one laboured to get forward; and...there was many time much quarrelling and fighting. But after every one had taken his place in the Caravan, they orderly and peaceably kept the same place till they came to Grand Cairo. They travel four camels in a breast, which are all tied one after the other, like as in teams. The whole body is called a Caravan, which is divided into several cottors, or companies, each of which hath its name, and consists, it may be, of several thousand camels; and they move one cottor after another, like distinct troops.

In the head of each cottor is some great gentleman or officer, who is carried in a thing like a horse-litter, borne by two camels, one before and the other behind, which is covered all over with...cloth, and set forth very handsomely....

Takht-rawans like this one were specially decorated litters for the rich and powerful to ride in. (From Richard F. Burton, *Personal Narrative of a Pilgrimage to Al-Madinah & Mecca,* Vol. I, 1893 ed.)

In the head of every cottor there goes, likewise, a sumpter camel which carries his treasures, etc. This camel hath two bells, about the bigness of our market-bells, having one on each side, the sound of which may be heard a great way off.

Some other of the camels have round bells about their necks, some about their legs...which together with the servants (who belong to the camels, and travel on foot) singing all night, make a pleasant

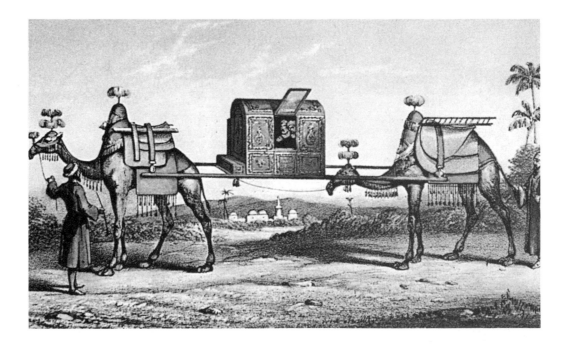

noise, and the journey passes away delightfully. They say this musick [sic] makes the camels brisk and lively.

The organization of the caravan was especially important because the caravan traveled mostly at night, as Pitts described:

> They have lights by night (which is the chief time of travelling, because of the exceeding heat of the sun by day), which are carried on the tops of high poles, to direct the Hagges [pilgrims] on their march. They are somewhat like iron stoves, into which they put short dry wood, which some of the camels are loaded with.

Besides light, these lamps provided information about each company: its size and camping place.

In the morning, after the long night's travel, the caravans usually pitched their tents, which took several hours. The camels were unloaded and taken for water by their owners, while the other travelers rested and ate. Sometimes the caravan would rest for short periods on the road, and when it was time to stop or start walking, a special gun would be fired.

Pitts said that his caravan did not pass near any settlements. In their 40 days' journey, he found "there is scarce any green thing to be met with, nor beast nor fowl to be seen or heard; nothing but sand and stones, excepting one place which we passed through by night; I suppose it was a village, which were some trees, and, we thought, gardens."

Even though the caravans didn't pass through any towns, they could still receive supplies along the route. Food was brought to them by little supply caravans that came from settled areas to meet them. Sometimes these supply caravans were joined by greeting parties, especially near the main caravan centers. Pitts described this:

> When we had taken our leave of Medina…and traveled about ten days more, we were met by a great many Arabians, who brought abundance of fruit to us, particularly raisins; but from whence I cannot tell. When we came within fifteen days' journey of Grand Cairo, we were met by many people who came from thence, with their camels laden with presents for the Hagges [pilgrims], sent from their friends and relations, as sweetmeats, etc. But some of them came rather for profit, to sell fresh provision to the Hagges, and trade with them….
>
> When we came within seven days' journey of Cairo, we were met by abundance of people more, some hundreds, who came to welcome

their friends and relations; but it being night, it was difficult to find those they wanted, and, therefore, as the Caravan past [sic] along they kept calling them aloud by their names, and by this means found them out. And when we were in three days' journey of it, we had many camel-loads of the water of the Nile brought us to drink. By the day and night before we came to Cairo, thousands came out to meet us with extraordinary rejoicing.

An Islam Reform Movement

In the mid-1700s a reform movement arose in central Arabia, aimed at bringing back "purity" to Islam. A man called Muhammad ibn 'Abd al-Wahab was convinced that reform was needed. He and his followers, who included the Saudi family, created a new movement—the Wahabis. The Wahabi movement spread quickly. In the early 1880s, the Wahabis even took the cities of Mecca and Medina, where they destroyed everything that they considered impure. Under Saudi leadership, the Wahabis then pushed into Syria and Iraq and east to Oman.

The Wahabis were not stopped until 1818, when the Ottoman Turks finally defeated them. The Turks opposed the Wahabis because the Wahabis had began to invade the Turkish Empire.

The Wahabis may have lost this battle, but their movement was not crushed. Their ideas spread throughout the Islamic world. These were years of great turmoil along the Pilgrimage Road. Finally, the Wahabis were defeated, and peaceful travel returned to the Pilgrimage Road.

European Travel in the Middle East

Charles Doughty. Englishman and explorer Charles M. Doughty described what Damascus (in modern Syria) was like in the 1870s as that city prepared for the departure of its annual caravan:

In the markets there is much taking up in haste of wares for the road. The tent-makers are most busy in their street, overlooking and renewing the old canvas of hundreds of tents...and the curtains for litters; the curriers in their bazaar are selling apace the water-skins and leathern buckets and saddle-bottles...; the carpenters' craft are labouring in all haste for the Haj [pilgrimage], the most of them mending litter-frames...the Haj caravan drivers...hold insolently their path through the narrow bazaars; commonly ferocious young men, whose mouths are full of horrible cursings....The *Mukowwems* or Haj camel-drivers...are sturdy, weathered men of the road, that can hold the mastery over their often mutinous crews....It is the custom of these caravan countries that all who are to set forth, meet together in some common place without [outside of] the city.

Doughty estimated that the pilgrimage he accompanied had 6,000 people, more than half of them servants on foot. There were also 10,000 animals, mostly camels, but also some mules and asses. For such a large number of people and animals, the start of the trip was surprisingly well organized:

The day risen the tents were dismantled, the camels led in ready to their companies, and halted beside their loads. We waited to hear the cannon shot which should open that year's pilgrimage. It was near ten o'clock when we heard the signal gun fired, and then, without any disorder, litters were suddenly heaved and braced upon the bearing beasts, their charges laid upon the kneeling camels, and the thousands of riders, all born in the caravan countries, mounted in silence. As all is up the drivers are left standing upon their feet, or set to rest out the latest moment on their heels: they with other camp and tent servants must ride those three hundred leagues upon their bare soles, although they faint; and are to measure the ground again upward with their weary feet from the holy places. At the second gun, fired a few moments after, the Pasha's [leader's] litter advances and after him goes the head of the caravan column: over fifteen or twenty minutes we, who have places in the rear, must halt, that is until the long train is unfolded before us; then we strike our camels and the great pilgrimage is moving. There go commonly three or four camels abreast and seldom five; the length of the slow-footed multitude of men and cattle is near two miles, and the width some hundred yards in the open plains.

The first day of the caravan was usually a short one, for neither pilgrim nor camels were yet used to the hardships of the road. At the desert station that night, the pilgrims found their tents already set up. Servants had hurried on ahead to prepare the night's camp. This they would do for the entire trip.

At night, armed guards circled the camp, keeping it safe. Pilgrims ate a meal cooked on a fire in a scooped-out hole, then relaxed—some with "drumbeating and soft fluting, and Arcadian sweetness of the Persians singing in the tents," others by chanting prayers by the light of a candle in a paper lantern.

The early part of the route was "a waste plain of gravel and loam upon limestone," according to Doughty. He said the route continued like that for 10 or 12 days.

Doughty found that there was no distinct road. Instead, there was only "a beaten way over the wilderness, paved of old at the crossing of winter stream-beds for the safe passage of the Haj camels, which have no foothold in sliding ground; by some other are seen ruinous bridges...." It was not only the bridges that had been ruined. The fortified way-stations and the towns themselves were often gone to ruin. Doughty described el Hejr, which had once been a caravan city: "her clay-built streets are again the blown dust in the wilderness..."

Richard Burton's Journey. Even in the 19th century, non-Moslems were still barred from Mecca. They had to disguise themselves as Moslems if they wanted to see the Moslem holy places and rituals.

The famous 19th-century traveler Richard P. Burton disguised himself as a Moslem doctor from India so he could join a pilgrimage. The caravan he joined waited in Medina for the great caravans to arrive from the north. From the house where he was staying, Burton awoke to find the Damascus caravan had arrived during the night:

[The field] from a dusty waste dotted with a few Badawi [Bedouin, or nomad] hair-tents, had assumed all the various shapes and the colours of a kaleidoscope....In one night had sprung up a town of tents of every size, colours, and shape; round, square, and oblong; open and closed,—from the shawl-lined and gilt-topped pavilion of the Pasha...to its neighbour the little dirty green "rowtie" of the tobacco-seller. They were pitched in admirable order: here ranged in a long line, where a street was required; there packed in dense masses, where thoroughfares were unnecessary. But how describe the utter confusion in the crowding, the bustling and the vast variety and volume of sound? Huge white Syrian dromedaries [camels], compared with which those of Al-Hijaz appeared mere pony-camels, jingling large bells, and bearing Shugdufs [litters] like miniature green tents, swaying and tossing upon their backs; gorgeous Takht-rawan, or litters carried between camels or mules with scarlet and brass trappings; Badawin bestriding naked-backed "Daluls" [camels], and clinging...to the hairy humps...fainting Persian pilgrims, forcing their stubborn camels to kneel, or dismounted grumbling from jaded donkeys; Kahwajis, sherbet sellers, and ambulant tobacconists crying their goods; country-people driving flocks of sheep and goats with infinite clamour through lines of horses fiercely snorting and biting and kicking and rearing; townspeople seeking their friends; returned travelers exchanging affectionate salutes...servants seeking their masters, and masters their tents, with vain cries of Ya Mohammed; grandees riding mules or stalking on foot, preceded by their crowd-beaters, shouting to clear the way...add a thick dust which blurs the outlines like a London fog, with a flaming sun that draws sparkles of fire from the burnished weapons of the crowd, and the brass balls of tent and litter.

The caravan on the move was even more remarkable than the tent city Burton had seen when he awoke. Here's his description of the traveling caravan:

The appearance of the Caravan was most striking, as it threaded its slow way over the smooth surface of the Khabt (low plain). To judge by the eye, the host was composed of at fewest seven thousand souls, on foot, on horseback, in litters, or bestriding the splendid camels of Syria.

There were eight gradations of pilgrims. The lowest hobbled with heavy staves [staffs, or walking sticks]. Then came the riders of asses, of camels, and of mules. Respectable men, especially Arabs, were mounted on dromedaries, and the soldiers had horses: a led animal was saddled for every grandee, ready whenever he might wish to leave his litter. Women, children, and invalids of the poorer classes sat upon a "Haml Musattah,"—rugs and cloths spread over the two large boxes which form the camel's load. Many occupied Shibriyahs; a few, Shugdufs, and only the wealthy and the noble rode in Takht-rawan (litters), carried by camels or mules.

The morning beams fell brightly upon the glancing arms which surrounded the stripped Mahmil and upon the scarlet and gilt conveyances of the grandee. Not the least beauty of the spectacle was its wondrous variety of detail: no man was dressed like his neighbour, no camel was caparisoned, no horse was clothed in uniform, as it were. And nothing stranger than the contrasts; a band of half-naked Takruri [African Moslems] marching with the Pasha's equipage, and long-capped bearded Persians conversing with Tarbush'd and shaven Turks.

The pilgrimages of the 1800s were little changed from those of the past. The caravans still combined religion and trading, and still needed supplies from both Jidda and Aden. But that was soon to change.

This valley on the Pilgrimage Road near Mecca was called the "Pass of Death" because pilgrims were in so much danger from robbers here. (From Richard F. Burton, *Personal Narrative of a Pilgrimage to Al-Madinah & Mecca*, Vol. II, 1893 ed.)

MODERN TIMES

European Empires. By the mid-1800s a few European nations dominated much of the world, either through controlling other nations as colonies or through the economic power of manufacture and trade. For several centuries, the Europeans had been trading in the East independently instead of depending on Moslem, Greek, and Indian traders.

The Moslems had tried to keep Europeans out of trade in the Red Sea. To some extent, they had been successful, although Europeans had tried several times to take the port of Aden (in today's country of Yemen). The Ottoman empire, based in Turkey, had also helped to counterbalance European power.

But by the second half of the 1800s, the Ottoman Turks had grown relatively weak, and more Europeans moved in to take control of large parts of the Middle East—Egypt, Syria, and Palestine (see Chapter 2). The Europeans also constructed the Suez Canal which joined the Mediterranean and the Red Seas. The Suez Canal became one of the world's great shipping lanes—and drew more Europeans to the region.

Railroads. European technology also reached inland. Between 1900 and 1908, the Turks, with German help, built the famous Hejaz Railway. The route they chose for it was the old Pilgrimage Road from Damascus to Medina, a distance of 800 miles.

Until the beginning of World War I, the pilgrimages continued—but now pilgrims simply piled into railroad cars for a four-day or even a three-day ride. Some of these railroad cars were open, but the hardships were still far less severe than those of a desert crossing. The old caravan stations on the route were converted into train stations.

A continuing hardship was fear of attack by the Bedouins, the nomadic traders who lived in the desert. These desert Arabs were generally anti-Turkish and antirailroad. Much of their income had come from renting camels to pilgrims, so they resented the railroad that took this income away. Indeed, they were the ones who stopped the railway line from being extended all the way to Mecca.

World War I. In 1914, World War I broke out. Bedouin discontent found a new outlet during World War I. The Wahabi reform movement had been reborn, and the British chose to support it because of its anti-Turkish tendencies. The British wanted to erode Turkish influence in the Middle East. The Turkish railroad continued to be a prime target for attacks. Southern parts of the line were destroyed by Arab forces inspired by the famous leader Lawrence of Arabia whose forces crossed the Nefud Desert to launch a surprise attack on Aqaba. Believing no one could cross the Nefud Desert, the Turks had not prepared for an attack from that direction. All the guns of Aqaba faced out to sea.

Modern States. After the war, the Saudi people came to power, creating the modern state of Saudi Arabia. They, too, opposed the

Many of the supply forts that line the Pilgrimage Road were later converted to railroad stations after the Hejaz Railway was built. (By Jacob M. Landau, from *The Hejaz Railway and the Muslim Pilgrimage,* reprinted by permission of Wayne State University Press)

railroad. They demanded that the other Moslem nations help pay for its repair, since they did not want to pay for it themselves. The result was that nothing was done. The Hejaz Railway was never reopened below the city of Ma'an in modern Jordan.

But the great pilgrimage caravans did not return. Pilgrims still made the journey to Mecca—but instead traveled on sea routes. They took ships through the Suez Canal to Yanbu', the port of Medina, or to Jidda, the port of Mecca.

Both Syria and northern Arabia had depended on pilgrimage trade for centuries. Now they were bypassed. They became poorer, and the old Pilgrimage Road fell into disuse.

Oil. In our time, oil has made Arabia far richer than either incense or the pilgrimages and has brought considerable wealth and status to the Middle Eastern states.

The Saudis have built a 40-square-mile international airport near Jidda. Now there are over 2 million pilgrims to Mecca every year, but they can fly over the harsh deserts and over the modern borders that divide today's Moslem nations.

Today's long-distance travel is mainly in the air. But down on the roads, next to the modern automobile, you can still see people traveling in the age-old way—by camel.

In modern Arabia, camel caravans sometimes tread on paved highways, like this one on a Jidda thoroughfare. (From Richard H. Sanger, *The Arabian Peninsula,* Cornell University Press)

Burton, Richard F. *Personal Narrative of a Pilgrimage to Al-Madinah & Meccah*, in two volumes (New York: Dover, 1964). Reprint of 1893 Memorial Edition published by Tylston and Edwards. A classic; the edition includes selections from earlier first-hand accounts as well.

Doughty, Charles M. *Travels in the Arabia Deserta* (Cambridge: At the University Press, 1888). A classic travel account.

Grant, Christina Phelps. *The Syrian Desert: Caravans, Travel and Exploration* (New York: Macmillan, 1938). Contains useful sections on the inland highway from Arabia.

Groom, Nigel. *Frankincense and Myrrh: A Study of the Arabian Incense Trade* (London: Longman, 1981). An extremely useful study of the early trade.

Hourani, George Fadlo. *Arab Seafaring: In the Indian Ocean in Ancient and Early Medieval Times* (New York: Octagon, 1975). Reprint of 1951 edition of Volume 13 of Princeton Oriental Studies. Includes useful information about associated land routes.

Huzayyin, S. A. *Arabia and the Far East: Their Commercial and Cultural Relations in Graeco-Roman and Irano-Arabian Times* (Cairo: Publications de la Societe Royale de Geographie D'Egypte, 1942). Includes coverage of the Incense Road as part of its wider treatment.

al-Munayyir, Muhammad 'Arif ibn Ahmad. *The Hejaz Railway and the Muslim Pilgrimage: A Case of Ottoman Political Propaganda*. Translated and edited by Jacob M. Landau. (Detroit: Wayne State University Press, 1971). A commentary on the hajj at the time the railway was built.

Rostovtzeff, M. *Caravan Cities* (Oxford: Clarendon Press, 1932). Contains a historical survey of the caravan trade plus accounts of visits to the ruined cities.

Sanger, Richard H. *The Arabian Peninsula* (Ithaca, New York: Cornell University Press, 1954). A view of the region in the 20th century.

Schreiber, Hermann. *The History of Roads: From Amber Route to Motorway* (London: Barrie & Rockliff, 1961). Translated from the German. Contains a chapter on the Incense and Pilgrimage Road.

Stark, Freya. *The Southern Gates of Arabia* (Los Angeles: J. P. Tarcher, 1976). Reprint of 1936 edition. Memoirs of a European woman traveling on the southern Incense Road in the 1930s.

5

THE SAHARA ROUTES: EARLY HISTORY

The Largest Desert in the World. The Sahara is the largest desert in the world. Named from the Arab word *sahra*, meaning wilderness, this huge mass of land takes up approximately three-and-a-half million square miles. The Sahara dominates northern Africa, where it runs 3,000 miles from the Atlantic Ocean to the Red Sea and ranges from 800 to 1,200 miles deep into the continent.

The Sahara comprises many diverse regions. There are vast areas of sand and sand dunes. These dunes can move dangerously in the wind, shifting to cover everything in their path. These sandy regions occupy much less than half of the Sahara's total territory. The Sahara also includes mountains as high as 8,000 feet and sometimes capped with snow. Two of the main mountain groups are the Tibesti Massif in the east-central Sahara and the Ahaggar Mountains in the west-central region. Other parts of the Sahara consist of hard-packed ground covered with loose gravel. Yet other parts are almost uncrossable regions of blackened rocks and boulders. Slicing through these rocks are deep-cut *wadis*, or water channels, that are prone to flash flooding. Sometimes floods come so suddenly that they can actually drown people who are standing in the streambed.

This vast desert is dotted with only a few dozen main oases. Often, palm trees and other fruit-bearing plants may grow around an oasis.

Frequently, people form settlements at oases and sell supplies to travelers who come through the desert looking for water. Most of the Sahara's oases are in the north-central part of the desert. Other parts of the Sahara have no oases at all. These are "deserts within the desert." The central Sahara, for example, is a gravel wasteland that may not have any rain at all for years at a time.

Trade in the Sahara. Despite the hostile conditions of the desert, througout history, people have found ways of traveling long distances across the desert to trade goods and information. Even in the Sahara, trade routes were used to transport salt, gold, and slaves north from the southern part of Africa and timber, ivory, and ostrich feathers south from the northern part of Africa.

People continually found creative ways of traveling through the desert. When camels were tamed, desert travel was made a great

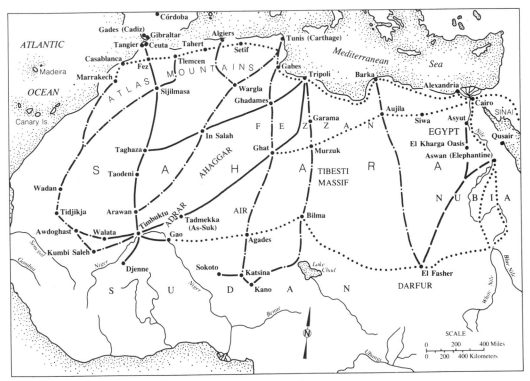

The Sahara Routes in the Late Middle Ages

———— Main Gold and Slave Routes
—·—· Other Main Trans-Sahara Routes
——— Derib el Arba'in (Track of the 40 Days)
········ Main Connecting Routes

deal easier, since camels could travel long distances with very little water. Aqueducts and dams could be used to collect water in key places along the road. Some peoples, such as the Romans, built roads into the desert. Other peoples, such as the Berbers, depended on caravan trails.

The harsh geography of the Sahara created a constant struggle for those who wished to trade there. Yet somehow, trade continued. The story of that trade—and that struggle—is the story of the Sahara Routes.

THE SAHARA IN EARLY TIMES

Fishing in the Desert. The Sahara has not always had the same geography as it has today. During the earth's existence, there have been many changes in the climate and the geography of its surface. Today the Sahara is one of the most desolate places in the world. But in the past, its climate was much moister and more able to support plant and animal life.

We know that the Sahara has changed because of the objects archaeologists found in the desert. For example, fishhooks and bone harpoon points have been found in the southwest quarter of the Sahara. This suggests that this area once included lakes and rivers where people fished and harpooned water animals.

In the central and northern Sahara, archaeologists have found life-size rock carvings that date back as far as 5000 B.C. They picture animals who could not live there in the present day, including the elephant, rhinoceros, and hippopotamus. Later rock carvings show domestic cattle. This suggests that the Sahara used to be a much richer and more fertile region.

The Climate Changes. Then, sometime between 3000 and 1500 B.C., a climate change must have occurred. All the lakes and swamps that once existed dried up. Eventually, many animals became extinct in the Sahara, and many forests died out.

The size and harshness of the desert increased, even as it continues to increase today. By the time the Mesopotamians (people from an ancient culture located in today's country of Iraq) and Europeans arrived on the scene, the Sahara was much as it is today, though a little smaller. However, the Maghreb—the belt of land that borders the Mediterranean just above the Sahara—was more lush than it is today and had more animals, including elephants, lions, leopards, and ostriches.

Early Trade and Travel

Nomads and Traders. We know very little about early travel across the Sahara. Most likely, it has not changed much through the years. In the warm season, desert nomads probably left their dried-up wells and pastures and headed out of the desert with their herds of oxen. *Nomads* means "wanderers," and these nomads had to wander in order to find fresh water and pasture for their herds.

The desert could support herds during the rainy season. But in the warm season, many nomads headed north to the Atlas Mountains or to the uplands of Algeria and Tunisia. Other nomads headed south to the Sudan, especially to the Niger Valley and Lake Chad. These other places had cooler weather and more vegetation to feed the herds.

Salt, Gold, and Slaves. Many centuries later, gold and slaves were traded from central and southern Africa for salt from the north. These were the early items of trade along the Sahara Routes.

We don't know when salt caravans first began crossing the Sahara. We do know that the earliest routes seem to have followed streambeds or run alongside hills. That way, traders could stay as close as possible to water and pasture for themselves and their

Sandstorms were always a major hazard in the Sahara, against which travelers protected their faces. (From James Richardson, *Travels in the Great Desert of the Sahara*, 1848)

animals. When the pack animals were oxen and horses, it was especially important to stay near water and fodder, or animal food.

Then, at some point, the caravan routes began to angle toward the main salt mines, deep in the Sahara Desert. In the west, they went to the old mines at Taghaza, north of Timbuktu, in the modern country of Mali. In the east, they headed for Bilma, in today's country of Niger. We don't know, however, whether any early traffic went all the way across the Sahara.

PEOPLES OF THE SAHARA

Different Peoples. Even in these early times, there were many peoples in the Sahara. There were two main groups. One was a dark-skinned Negroid group. They descended from immigrants who had pushed north from the Sudan into the Sahara as early as 3000 B.C. and were generally known to the Europeans as Ethiopians. They were said to occupy all the land south of Libya. The other main group was the light-skinned peoples of North Africa and the west and central Sahara. The Greeks called these Libyans, but the Romans called them *barbari*, meaning "barbarians." From this Roman name came the regional name "Barbary." Later, Europeans called these people Berbers.

The Phoenicians Arrive. In about 1000 B.C., foreigners came to Barbary, bringing widespread changes. The first foreigners to come were the Phoenicians.

The Phoenicians founded their first empire in the area roughly corresponding to the coast of present-day Lebanon. They were expert sailors and navigators and knew a great deal about the seaways around them.

The Phoenicians founded colonies in the ports they visited. One colony, located near modern Tripoli in Libya, they called Leptis Magna. Another colony, in present-day Tunisia, they called Carthage. By about 500 B.C., these colonies had joined together to become an independent empire. The capital of this new empire was Carthage. Eventually the Phoenicians became known as the Carthaginians.

Leptis Magna was important as a seaport but also as the end-point of a land route—the Garamantes road. This road led through Fezzan, known as Phazania in that time, in the north Sahara.

It is not known exactly what goods were carried along this road in early days. They many have included skins, timber, ivory, ostrich feathers, gold, or slaves, for all these products were traded along this road in later times. Another trade item that several early writers mention is the carbuncle, an unknown kind of stone. Some think carbuncles were beads of chalcedony, a quartz-like stone from the west coast of Africa thought to have mystical powers. If so, carbuncles might have been the earliest items to be shipped routinely all the way across the Sahara to foreign traders.

ROMAN TIMES

The Romans Invade. At around the time of Christ, the Romans took over the Carthaginians' Barbary colonies and installed their own headquarters near Carthage. They called the area Provincia Africa, the province of Africa.

The Carthaginians had settled mainly on the North African coast. But the Romans went inland. They wanted to extend their territory along the hills of North Africa. This brought them into direct contact with the nomads of the north Sahara when those nomads moved their herds into the hills for the summer. The Romans tried to hold the nomads back by putting groups of soldiers at each oasis along the main routes that led into the north Sahara. However, they were not successful at holding the nomads back. The Romans then sent an army into the heart of the Fezzan. That worked better for them. With surprise on their side, the Romans easily took the main Fezzan oases.

But their victory was short-lived. Soon the Roman army had to withdraw to a line that it could defend. They had to pull back for a 30-day march over the almost waterless desert.

The people who lived in that area were called the Garamantes. They were surprised that the Romans had been able to invade territory they had thought was secure. Even though the Roman invasion had failed, the Garamantes did not want to risk another invasion. So they filled up all the wells in the area with sand.

Camels. The situation eased when camels were brought into the Maghreb—the Mediterranean coastal strip of North Africa. Camels had reached Egypt as early as the 6th century B.C., and they were in the eastern Sudan before the time of Christ. But they reached the

Maghreb only around the Christian era. They were introduced either by the Romans or by Berber nomads who were pushing along the coast from the east.

Camels made a huge difference to this desert region, for they made travel much easier. Unlike other animals, camels can endure long periods of time without water, and can tolerate high temperatures. If humans could carry enough water for themselves, they could ride their camels across the desert. However, some areas in the Sahara were too harsh and barren even for camels.

The Romans and the Garamantes eventually became allies, which enabled the Romans to build new roads in the area. These were probably cross-desert routes that could not have been used before the days of camels.

Rome's Changes. Along with the Romans, other Europeans and Asians also seem to have reached into the Sahara in the centuries after Christ. They may even have reached into the Sahara to settle deep into Africa.

Roman rule brought some destructive changes to the Sahara region. They hunted many animals in Libya, and, as a result of this early hunting, many of these animals are now extinct or nearly extinct. For example, the small North African elephant is now extinct. The breed of lion that flourished in that area was also hunted to extinction. Hundreds of these lions were shipped from Leptis Magna to Ostia, the port of Rome. The Romans made sport of lions battling with gladiators, slaves who were specially trained in the art of combat. Many lions were killed this way.

The Romans also brought some improvements to the region. Their building and engineering work helped North Africans make the most of precious water in the area. Distant springs were tapped and water brought to Roman areas by great aqueducts, huge pipes that carried water over long distances. One such aqueduct brought water to Carthage from nearly 90 miles away.

The Romans also built dams across the wadis, so that whatever rain fell could be collected in reservoirs. Smaller amounts of water were collected in cisterns, or water tanks, in the hills and even on the roofs of private houses.

These supplies of water helped the peoples of Roman Africa to expand, using irrigation to convert desert into good land. These engineering advances helped the towns and the northern desert oases to prosper for many centuries, even after Roman power declined.

North African elephants and other wild beasts were loaded on boats like these and shipped across the Mediterranean to Italy for the bloody Roman games. (Drawing from a mosaic in the Piazza Amerina, about A.D. 300)

Roman Roads and Caravan Trails. Throughout this period, the Romans focused their attention on the eastern Maghreb. They built roads from 8- to 22-feet-wide, mainly along the Mediterranean coast, from the Atlantic Ocean to Egypt. They also built roads inland from Carthage, especially to the market towns where the nomads traded.

But beyond the Roman roads were the caravan trails. Many of these were set up by the Berbers. With camels, they had moved into the Sahara from the east over several centuries. They conquered many oases and mountain regions held by Negroid peoples and reached as far as the Niger River.

In the Moslem World

Arabs in Africa. Eventually, Roman power declined, and in the late 7th century, Arabs entered the Sahara, bringing with them their new religion of Islam. The Romans had focused their attention on the Maghreb, mainly the areas that today are part of Libya and

Tunisia. The Arab Moslems moved across the Maghreb to the Atlantic. At this time, however, the Berbers revolted. They destroyed the new Arab capital of Kairouan in Tunisia and drove the Arabs all the way back to Egypt. For a time it looked as though Islam would not take hold in North Africa.

Then, in the early 8th century, the Arabs returned. They rebuilt Kairouan, converted many Berbers to Islam, and headed across the Strait of Gibralter to take Spain. The Europeans called these invaders "Moors."

Many Arabs settled in the fertile, well-watered land of the western Maghreb, where they built a lively, growing culture. They drew on the learning and skills of the great Mediterranean peoples and on a flow of settlers ranging from farmers to scholars. Many of these settlers came from Spain.

ARAB TRADING

The Arabs Expand Trade. The Arabs transformed the simple trade of the Sahara. In the 8th century, the kingdom of Ghana, west of the Niger River in modern Mali, monopolized the gold and salt trade of the region. A trade route ran between Ghana's capital of Kumbi and the Berber-controlled salt mines at Taghaza, a 20-day march north.

The Arabs had always thrived on trade. Now they moved to expand it. In the 8th century, they built a post at Sijilmasa, an oasis just south of the Atlas Mountains.

Sijilmasa was close enough to the Taghaza salt mines that traders from Sijilmasa could deal in salt. They took that salt to Ghana where they exchanged it for gold. An anonymous 12th century Moslem author described this trade:

> In the sands of that country [Ghana] is gold, and the merchants trade with salt for it, taking the salt on camels from the salt mines. They start from a town called Sijilmasa...and travel in the desert as it were upon the sea, having guides to pilot them by the stars or rocks in the deserts. They take provisions for six months, and when they reach Ghana, they weigh their salt and sell it against a certain unit of weight of gold, and sometimes against double or more of the gold unit, according to the market and the supply.

Ghana itself did not produce the gold; it came from a country called Wangara. But Wangara's location was secret. Some Arabs even attacked Ghana in the middle of the 8th century, hoping to find out where the gold was located, but the attack failed.

A Rival Market. To the west of Ghana was a rival kingdom of Sanhaja Berbers. This people had once lived in the Sahara but had moved farther south. Centuries later, the Europeans misunderstood their name. The mispronounced European word was used to identify the river that watered this land—the Senegal.

The Sanhaja set up a rival market at Awdoghast, a 15-day march west of Kumbi. Both Kumbi and Awdoghast housed Arab merchants. These merchants generally lived apart from the local people in neighborhoods of their own.

Trade prospered on the caravan route north to Sijilmasa. Despite frequent fighting among these rivals, trade remained steady. Often, opposing sides would call a truce, so that a market could be opened.

A Silent Trade. The trade itself was somewhat unusual. Arab traders would leave Sijilmasa with cheap goods, like coral beads. They would trade these for salt on their way through Taghaza, where the salt mines were located. Finally, the Arabs would arrive in Kumbi, where they were joined by agents from Ghana who took them on a 20-day march southwest to the Senegal. At the Senegal, the Arabs and Ghanaians beat drums to announce their arrival. The Arab merchants spread their goods out on the river bank. Then they left.

Only when the Arabs had gone would the local people come out. The local people would place on the riverbanks an amount of gold that they thought was equal to the value of the goods the Arabs had left for them. If the Arabs agreed, they would take the gold and leave, beating the drums to signal that they had accepted. If they did not agree, they might take back some of their goods. Then they would leave for a short time while the local people came back to accept this deal or to adjust their own offer.

This silent trade continued for many centuries. For the local people, it had the advantage of protecting the source of their gold. Many outsiders tried to discover this secret but never succeeded.

Slave Trade. Arabs on the Sahara route were in search of more than gold. Merchants from new cities, like Fez, were looking for slaves. Ghana captured slaves through raids on the forest which bordered the Sudan. Then they sold these people to the Arabs.

Oases. The Sahara's trade was active but also quite dangerous. Any trip across the wasteland could offer new problems, no matter how many caravans had gone before. It was possible that an oasis might have dried up between one trip and the next. Even as late as 1805, lack of water led to the deaths of 2,000 men and 1,800 camels in a caravan traveling home to Fez from Timbuktu.

One oasis might be a week's journey away from the next. When a caravan did arrive at an oasis, there was a flurry of activity, as the people who lived there rushed to sell goods to the travelers. Here is the description of Rene Caillie. He was writing in the 19th century, but he might just as easily have been describing the arrival of a caravan at a desert well a thousand years earlier:

Rene Caillie's sketch of Timbuktu makes clear how barren its setting was. (From *Journal d'un Voyage a Temboctou et a Jenne dans l'Afrique Centrale,* 1830)

In the midst of this vast desert, the wells of Mourat, surrounded by fourteen hundred camels and by the four hundred men of our caravan, who were crowded round them, presented the moving picture of a populous town; it was a perfect turmoil of men and beasts. On the

one side were camels laden with ivory, and bales of goods of all sorts; on the other, camels carrying on their back [slaves]...men, women and children, who were on their way to be sold at the Morocco markets; further on, men prostrate [stretched out] on the ground, invoking the Prophet.

The Selling of Slaves. Arabs also settled farther east in the Maghreb. They often intermarried with Jewish settlers who lived at the oases. Like the Arabs farther west, they also joined the slave trade in the Sudan.

There were various routes on which slaves were traded, but all routes took the slaves north, up from the Sudan into the Maghreb. Some slaves were headed for the deadly work in the salt mines— backbreaking labor that could easily wear a person out in a few years. Other slaves labored in irrigated fields around the oases. The rest of the slaves were sold in the coastal cities, and from there European traders eventually began shipping them to the Americas, where they labored on huge plantations in South America, Central America, and the southern part of the United States.

Many slaves did not survive the march across the desert. Later travelers on these routes might find the bones of these slaves mixed with the bones of camels who had died on the trip.

The Spread of Islam

Pilgrimages. Trade with the north brought the peoples of the Sahara into contact with Islam. Senegal converted to this religion. So did the people of Tucolor of the Kingdom of Tukrar—the earliest dark-skinned converts. The Tucolor converts were the first West African people to make the *hajj*, or pilgrimage, to Mecca that every Moslem was supposed to make at least once in a lifetime.

Most of the other Moslem countries organized yearly pilgrimage caravans that journeyed to Mecca. The West African peoples had a different practice. Members of the royal families would go on a pilgrimage, sometimes more than once, and would be joined by hundreds or thousands of their people.

Some people wanted to make the journey without royal protection, however. These people either had to make up small caravans of their own or to join trading caravans. Whatever they chose, they had to join a caravan to cross the Sahara. It was too dangerous to make the journey without a large group.

A Long Journey. The pilgrimage was a long trip. Crossing the Sahara took two months. Thus, the pilgrimage was expensive, both in cash for supplies and in lost working time while on the journey. It was also a hard trip that required travelers to be in good physical condition.

As a result, very few West African Moslems made this journey in the early centuries. Local scholars in the region decided that this religious duty should not be required of everyone but only of those who were capable of making the trip. The royal, wealthy, or learned people who did go to Mecca often visited other famous Moslem cities along the way. Thus, they brought back to West Africa new ideas from other places.

The Almoravids. One Sanhaja chief brought back a learned Moslem, Abdullah ibn Yasin, to educate his people. However, ibn Yasin quickly founded a new Moslem group, the Almoravids. This group grew quickly and started a *jihad*, or holy war, to force other Moslems to convert to their sect of Islam.

The Almoravids became so strong that they attacked the Maghreb with an army of 30,000 men. They took Fez and founded the city of Marrakech, which the Europeans mispronounced as "Morocco." The Almoravids went on to take Moslem Spain.

In the south, the Almoravids attacked non-Moslems. In 1076, they took Kumbi, massacred its citizens, and forced the survivors to convert to Islam. But the Almoravids could not maintain control of Ghana and the rest of the southern Sahara, though they did remain strong in the north.

Changes in Trade Patterns. The fighting caused by the Almoravids led Arab traders to set up a new post in the early 1200s. The site they chose was 100 miles north of Kumbi at an old camping ground called Walata. Walata became the main trading center of the region, and Awdoghast and Kumbi both lost trade. Another reason for this shift was that the gold fields of the Senegal River were not as productive as those of the upper Niger River, which was closer to Walata.

Then Walata itself was replaced by Timbuktu as the main trading center in the western Sahara. Timbuktu had begun as a small camping ground a few centuries before. Traders had begun to go to this camping ground because it was just a few miles from both the Niger and the desert. There, both river and desert people could trade grain, kola nuts, and gold dust for northern goods, especially dates and salt.

By 1100, Timbuktu had become a small village of grass huts. Soon the small village had become a little town of sun-dried brick buildings. Timbuktu was located in the country of Mali. When the country of Ghana fell apart, the kingdom of Mali became the main trading nation in the area with Timbuktu as its trading and cultural center.

MANSA MUSA

In 1324, Mali caught the attention of the world. That was the year that Mali's king, Mansa Musa, made a pilgrimage to Mecca, and his spectacular display of wealth caused a great commotion among all those who heard about it. Mansa Musa took with him 500 slaves, each carrying a staff of gold. He rode on horseback, showering gold and costly gifts everywhere he went. Tales of this wealthy king spread throughout the world.

On his return home, Mansa Musa visited the town of Gao. This was the capital of the Songhai people of the middle Niger of which Mali had recently taken control. At Gao, Mansa Musa approved the building of a mosque, a Moslem holy building. The mosque was designed by a poet and architect named as-Sahili. It was made of burnt bricks, a new building method for the region. This building stood for 300 years, and its foundations remained strong into the 20th century.

BEDUOINS IN THE MAGHREB

The Growth of Mali. Eventually, Mali stretched its territory from the Atlantic coast to Walata. It included the desert market of Tadmekka and the upper and middle Niger River. Only the city of Djenne, on the upper Niger, kept its independence. Perhaps that was because Djenne was surrounded by waterways that helped protect the city from attack.

Bedouin Rulers. While Timbuktu and the kingdom of Mali were rising in the south, the peoples of the north saw new rulers. In the 11th century, the Bani Hilal, a group of Bedouin Arabs, swept into the Maghreb, destroying improvements as they went. Aqueducts, dams, and cisterns had kept many northern towns green and productive since Roman times. But the Bani Hilal destroyed them all. Now much of the land in the region could no longer be farmed.

Worse than that, these invaders were nomads, bringing large herds of animals with them. The herds destroyed much of the remaining forests and brush of the region. The Maghreb became much more like the desert and has remained that way ever since. Even some of the great seaports of early times, like Leptis Magna, have been buried by sand.

MOSLEM TRAVELERS

Ibn Battuta, Moslem Traveler. The Arab invasion destroyed much in the north. But it also opened a door to the East, and so began a great age of travel.

Earlier, West African kings had made the long pilgrimages to Mecca. Now these journeys were taken up by ordinary Moslems as well. One of the most famous Moslem travelers was known as Ibn Battuta who lived in the 14th century. He left many records of his journeys.

One such record is of a trip that Ibn Battuta made with a caravan that formed in Sijilmasa. This caravan was headed for the Sudan and had to pass through Taghaza. Ibn Battuta found that Taghaza was

> an unattractive village, with the curious feature that its houses and mosques are built of blocks of salt, roofed with camel skins. There are no trees there, nothing but sand. In the sand is a salt mine; they dig for the salt, and find it in thick slabs....No one lives at Taghaza except the slaves of the Mesufa tribe, who dig for the salt: they subsist on dates imported from Dra's and Sijilmasa, camel's flesh, and millet imported from the Negrolands [that is, the land where dark-skinned people lived, further south]...[The residents of that land]...come up from their country and take away the salt from there. At Walata a load of salt brings eight to ten mithgals [a mithgal is about 1/8 ounce of gold]; in the town of Mali it sells for twenty to thirty, and sometimes as much as forty. The...[local people] use salt as a medium of exchange, just as gold and silver is used [elsewhere]; they cut it up into pieces and buy and sell with it. The business done at Taghaza, for all its meanness, amounts of an enormous figure in terms of hundred-weights of gold-dust.

Leo Africanus. Another famous traveler, Leo Africanus (see Chapter 6), wrote a similar description over a century later:

> Neither have the said diggers of salt any victuals but such as the merchants bring unto them; for they are distant from all inhabited

places almost twenty days' journey, insomuch that oftentimes they perish [die] for lack of food whenas the merchants come not in due time unto them. Moreover, the southeast wind doth so often blind them, that they cannot live here without great peril. I myself continued three days amongst them, all which time I was constrained to drink salt-water drawn out of certain wells not far from the salt-pits.

Caravan Journeys. After leaving Taghaza, Ibn Battuta's caravan stopped at a waterhole for a few days. Here animals and people rested, and travelers mended the all-important water-skins which had to hold their water supply between wells.

Once the caravan got underway, they sent a special messenger called a *takshif* ahead to Walata. The messenger, traveling by himself on a fast horse, could reach the city more quickly and easily than the huge group of men and camels in the caravan. That was partly because the camels grazed as they traveled, so their speed was only about two miles an hour. The messenger arranged for water to be carried out to the caravan. If this were not done, some people might not survive the last few miles of the journey.

Surprisingly, sometimes the head *takshif* was blind, or nearly blind, even though it was his job to be pilot for the caravan. Imagine how difficult it would be to follow a route through the desert. Each landmark would look different on each trip because of the shifting sands. Yet both Ibn Battuta and Leo Africanus traveled with pilots who could not see well. Africanus described how his pilot found the way:

> [He rode] foremost on his camel, [and] commanded some sand to be given him at every mile's end, by the smell whereof he declared the situation of the place.

Caravans crossing in the heat of summer would often travel by night. Thus they avoided the worst of the sun's effects.

BEFORE THE EUROPEANS CAME

The world of Ibn Battuta was ruled by Arabs and Africans. Until the 15th century, these were the peoples who controlled the Sahara, North Africa, and the Middle East. In the 15th century, Europeans began coming to the region, seeking the gold they had heard about. Europeans were also searching for their own sea route to the Far East, where they hoped to trade in the valuable spices, silks, and jewels that had come to them from India, China, and the Spice Islands.

At first, the Europeans came as traders who were awed by the magnificent cities of Northern Africa. Eventually, however, the Portuguese, French, Dutch, and British took over huge portions of the continent and dominated the local trade. In any case, the coming of the Europeans drastically changed the history of the region.

6

THE SAHARA ROUTES: LATER HISTORY

THE EUROPEANS SEARCH FOR GOLD

For centuries, the people of Europe had coveted the goods that came to them from the Far East. The spices, silks, jewels, and porcelain were unlike any products that the Europeans had in their own countries. They needed to get these items from China, India, and the Far East.

Until the 15th century, the Europeans were dependent on Arab, Indian, and Greek sailors to carry Spice Route products from Asia to the Middle East. From the Middle East, these goods were then brought through the Red Sea and over land to the Mediterranean, from where they were shipped to European countries.

Initially, the Europeans couldn't travel to the Far East themselves because they didn't know the sea routes that led to the Far East. But in the 15th century, a great age of exploration began. European merchants and sailors explored the Red Sea and the coast of Africa, looking for the routes east.

The Europeans were also intent on finding the famous kingdoms of Africa. They had heard that these kingdoms were filled with golden cities and fabulous wealth. Travelers like Leo Africanus and Ibn Battuta had left written accounts of their journeys in Africa. There were also maps, drawn by Jewish mapmakers late in the 14th century, based on information from Jewish merchants traveling with caravans in the Sahara.

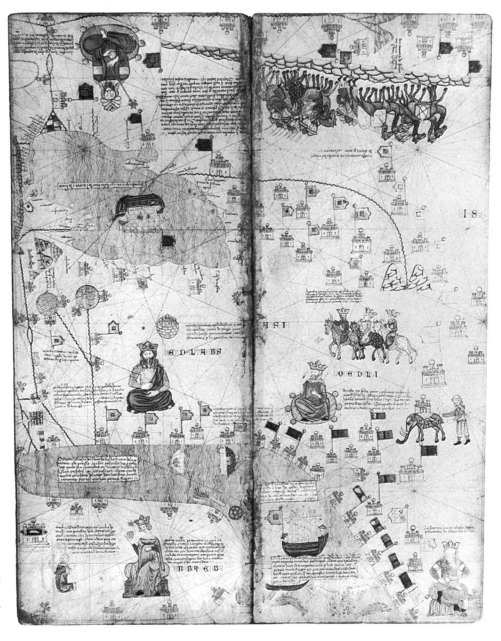

Early maps like this one, showing caravans in the desert, were drawn by Jewish mapmakers in Spain, using information from merchants. (From *Atlas Catalan*, 1375, Bibliotheque Nationale, Paris)

At first, the Europeans were quite ignorant about the African continent and the sea routes around it. Gradually, however, they began to learn more about it. And eventually they came to dominate Africa, both through trading with African nations and through actually taking over huge sections of Africa as colonies.

A View of Timbuktu. Leo Africanus' real name was Al Hassan ibn Mohammed Alwazan. But he was known in Europe as Leo Africanus, which in Latin means African lion. He traveled through the Sahara and then wrote about it in 1559. Here is his description of Timbuktu, a major trading city located in today's country of Mali:

> Here are many shops of…[craft workers] and merchants, and especially of such as weave linen and cotton cloth. And hither to the Barbarie merchants bring cloth of Europe. All the women of this region except maid-servants go with their faces covered.…The inhabitants, and especially strangers there residing, are exceedingly rich, insomuch that the king that now is, married both his daughters unto two rich merchants. Here are many wels [sic] containing most sweete [sic] water; and so often as the river Niger overfloweth they conveigh the water thereof by certain sluces [sluices, or drains] into the towne. Corne [grain], cattle, milke and butter this region yeeldeth in great abundance; but salt is scarce heere, for it is brought hither by land from Tegaza which is five hundred miles distant. When I myself was here, I saw one cammels loade of salt sold for 80 ducates.

The Trade in Gold. The Europeans had heard of a "golden trade" that Africans conducted across the Sahara to the Sudan. They were especially interested in Alwazan's description of Timbuktu's royal court:

> The rich king…hath many plates and scepters of gold, some whereof weigh 1,300 poundes: and he keepes a magnificent and well furnished court.

There were many other such stories about fabulously rich Moslem African princes. From these tales, Europeans built up a picture of Timbuktu as a golden city far richer than any they knew in their own countries.

In creating this image, they ignored the rest of Alwazan's story. He himself wrote that he had expected a much richer city. He was disappointed to note that "all the houses…are now changed into cottages built of chalke and covered with thatch."

If the city did not live up to its romantic image, it was still a major trading center. Alwazan noted:

> Here are great store of doctors, judges, priests, and other learned men, that are bountifully maintained at the king's cost and charges.

And hither are brought divers manuscripts or written books out of Barbarie, which are sold for more money than any other merchandise.

EUROPEANS IN AFRICA

What the Europeans Knew. Alwazan's description supported the European idea of Africa as a rich land full of golden cities. Even though this idea was somewhat exaggerated, there was some truth in it. At the time the Europeans first began to visit Africa in any great numbers, the Sahara in particular was the site of a rich caravan trade.

Europeans did have some information about Africa, primarily in the form of the maps made by Jewish mapmakers. These maps were crude, but they did show the cities of Timbuktu, Gao, and Mali, among others.

In the 15th century, some European sailors and merchants began exploring the coasts of Africa. Most were interested in working their way around this unknown continent so they could reach the Spice Routes of the Far East. But some of the merchants were more interested in exploring inland to see if they could find African gold.

They didn't get very far. The inland routes were then in the control of Barbary merchants who did not want any competitors for the gold mines of the Sudan.

Moslems, Christians, and Jews. Not all Europeans had been ignorant of Africa until the 15th century. Many Christian Europeans had lived in North Africa for centuries before. But although Christians and Jews lived in North Africa, the dominant religion in the region was Islam.

In the 15th century, religious conflicts between Christians and Moslems in North Africa were growing. Moslems vastly outnumbered Christians and could easily dominate them. Jews, meanwhile, suffered at the hands of both. Many Jews were massacred in the oases of the northern Sahara—even though their families had lived in these places for a thousand years or more.

Sea Routes. These conflicts made it dangerous for Christian Europeans to use Africa's land routes. But the sea routes were not in danger. Portuguese Christian explorers continued their search for the Spice Routes to the Far East on these sea routes as well as continuing their search for the West African gold fields.

Gradually, the Portuguese worked their way around the southern tip of Africa after many attempts. Each expedition that was sent took part in trading. At first, the Portuguese focused on slave trading. Slave traders in the port towns would offer slaves for sale to the Portuguese merchants who landed in their harbors. The Portuguese also sent scouts inland to look for gold.

The Portuguese slave trade made them extremely unpopular with the African people. Also, the diseases, insects, and snakes which the Portuguese encountered in coastal Africa diminished their desire to set up real trade routes into Africa's heartland. But Europe's desire for gold and slaves could still be satisfied by the coastal trade. So the caravans across the Sahara continued. These caravans brought goods—including gold and slaves—up from the areas that today are called the Sudan, Chad, Niger, and Mali. These goods were traded with North Africans and Europeans along the African coast.

European Christians, here shown in chains in Algiers, were sometimes captured in wars or pirate engagements and set to work as slaves in North African cities. (Engraving by P. Dan, British Library Board)

THE SONGHAI EMPIRE

Changes were taking place in the Sudan itself. The kingdom of Mali was threatened by the rising kingdom of Songhai on the middle Niger. First, the Songhai took back their capital city of Gao, winning it from the Mali people who had conquered it. Then, in 1468, the Songhai army seized the Mali city of Timbuktu. They killed many citizens to establish their rule. A few years later, they took the city of Djenne. This town had become an important center for European trade. Finally, they took the trading center of Walata.

When the Mandingo people of Mali asked the Portuguese to help them against the Songhai, the Portuguese refused. Thus Songhai power continued to increase in the area.

MOROCCAN CONQUEST

Moors and Sahara Gold. The Europeans were not the only ones who sought West African gold. The Moors, a North African people based in the area that today is known as Morocco, had for centuries been trading with caravans that traveled through the Sahara to receive the gold that arrived from the south. They depended on Sudanese traders to bring them this gold—but were always on the lookout for a way of getting it directly for themselves.

However, despite their desire for Sahara gold, they were afraid to invade the Sudan. For years, they had believed that it was impossible to invade the Sudan from across the desert. Then, in the second half of the 16th century, the Moroccan ruler al-Mansur acquired modern European firearms. With these guns, he decided to risk an invasion.

Al-Mansur's Invasion. Al-Mansur first focused on the salt mines of Taghaza. These mines were the key to the gold trade, since it was salt that was traded for the gold. The Songhai refused to give al-Mansur control of the Taghaza salt mines. So al-Mansur set out with his army to take it by force. But he found only an empty shell. The mines were there—but the local nomads and their African slaves had run away. The Songhai forbade them to return. These slaves were needed to work the mines. Al-Mansur had gained nothing, and he had caused the end of the Taghaza mines.

New Salt Mines. The Taureg nomads had been attacked by the Moors, and so were eager to help the Songhai, since the Songhai were under Moorish attack. Thus, they told the Songhai about another large salt deposit, about 100 miles to the south at Taodeni.

The Songhai went to the new salt deposit and started new mines. These new mines were closer to the surface and easier to work. The Taodeni mines are still being worked today, but the Taghaza mines never reopened.

Al-Mansur Attacks the Sudan. Al-Mansur was frustrated with his worthless victory at Taghaza. He decided to attack the Sudan itself, to go directly where he thought the gold mines were. His advisers all disagreed. But, according to the writer al-Ifrani, al-Mansur replied as follows:

> You talk of the dangerous desert we have to cross, of the fatal solitudes, barren of water and pasture, but you forget the defenseless and ill-equipped merchants who, mounted or on foot, regularly cross these wastes which caravans have never ceased to traverse. I, who am so much better equipped than they, can surely do the same with an army which inspires terror wherever it goes....Our predecessors would have found great difficulty if they had tried to do what I now propose, for their armies were composed only of horsemen armed with spears and of bowmen; gunpowder was unknown to them, and so were firearms and their terrifying effect. Today the Sudanese have only spears and swords, weapons which will be useless against modern arms. It will therefore be easy for us to wage a successful war against these people and prevail over them.

Al-Mansur won the argument with his counselors. They agreed to make the attack from the desert, but preparing for the attack was no easy matter. Up to this point, only small caravans had crossed the Sahara, and there was scarcely even enough water in the wells for them. How, then, could the wells supply enough water for the thousands of men in al-Mansur's army?

Al-Mansur decided that they would have to carry most of the food and water for the 1,500-mile journey. They took 8,000 camels, 100 camel-drivers, and 1,000 pack horses to carry their supplies.

The soldiers were from many lands because Morocco did not have a large population. There were Moroccan Moors, Spanish Moors, and European Christians, many of whom were mercenaries. The entire army consisted of 4,000 people: 2,000 in the cavalry and 2,000 in the infantry. All were armed with guns called *arquebuses*. There were also 600 sappers, whose work was to build and destroy military fortifications.

The camel-driver was always an important figure in the Sahara, for he ran the caravans that linked the Maghreb with distant Sudan. (Photo Garrigues, Tunis, from Norma Lorimer, *By the Waters of Carthage*, 1906)

The army also carried a huge amount of supplies: 31,000 pounds of gunpowder and 3,000 yards of English cloth "for lining the tents of the arquebusiers [the people who shot the arquebuses]..."

The Story of the Campaign. The army left Morocco at the best time for travel—in mid-October when the heat of the summer had subsided. Slowly, they worked their way to the southeast. First they stayed as close as possible along the foothills of the Atlas Mountains to be close to grassy land and water. Then, following the oases, they headed into the desert, looking for the main caravan route through Taghaza.

No records survive of what the march was like. But Leo Africanus had taken the same route earlier that century. He left us this description of the difficulties of the route:

In the way which leadeth from Fez to Timbuktu are certain pits environed with the hides or bones of camels. Neither do the merchants in summer pass that way without great danger of their lives:

for oftentimes it falleth out, when the south wind bloweth, that all these pits are stopped up with sand. And so the merchants, when they can find neither those pits, nor any mention thereof, must needs perish with extreme thirst: whose carcases are afterwards found lying scattered here and there, and scorched with the heat of the sun. One remedy they have in this case, which is very strange: for when they are so grievously oppressed with thirst, they kill forthwith some one of their camels, out of whose bowels they wring and express some quantity of water, which water they drink and carry with them, till they have either found some pit of water, or till they pine away for thirst.

Many of al-Mansur's army died in the desert. Only about 1,000 even went into the first battle with the Songhai. Perhaps some others of the original 4,000 did survive but were simply too weak or ill to fight in the first battle. Despite their reduced number, the Moors were victorious. Al-Mansur had been right in thinking that guns would make the difference. The Moors were outnumbered by over twenty to one, but they easily defeated the Songhai.

Nevertheless, the victory was hollow, just as the victory at Taghaza had been. Al-Mansur had expected Gao and Timbuktu to be great, golden cities. But their mud-and-thatch buildings looked very poor to Moorish eyes. Nor was there any gold to be found. In Gao, people had fled from the cities, taking almost every piece of gold with them.

New arms technology, imported from the Europeans, was adapted to the needs of the desert, as with this cannon slung on a camel's back. (From Diderot, *Encyclopedia*, late 18th century)

The War Continues.   It was hard for the Moors to keep control of the country after they had won it. War continued in the region for some years, and the Songhai and their allies were at least fighting on home ground, whereas the Moors had to get reinforcements from across the Sahara. The continuous fighting, however, badly damaged the centuries-old trading networks and alliances.

Finally, the Moors did find gold. In the middle of 1599, their army's leader, Judar, returned to Morocco with 30 camel-loads of unrefined gold. An English merchant then living in the city of Marrakech (Morocco) valued its worth at 604,800 pounds—a considerable amount of money. Judar also brought loads of other goods and many slaves. However, all this was scant reward for several years of heavy fighting.

The Songhai continued to send tribute to Morocco for many years. But after al-Mansur died, Morocco was torn by civil war, and the Moorish army was left isolated in the Sudan.

The Mandingo and other subject peoples took this opportunity to revolt. Gradually, from being conquerors, the Moors became integrated with the local population. They set up an elite called the Arma, made up of people from this mixed background.

The Arma ruled the region for two centuries. Finally, it, too, became fully integrated into the general population. Then trade resumed as before with only a few ties between Morocco and the Sudan. But as late as 1958, King Muhammed V of Morocco claimed that his country stretched across the Sahara to include Timbuktu.

Changes in the Sahara

A Different Group of Europeans.   For many years, Portugal had controlled the foreign trade of West Africa. But in the 16th century, the British Queen Elizabeth I made a deal for her country to sell arms to the Moroccans. From that time, the British began to replace the Portuguese. Other northern Europeans took over the slave trade, especially in the ports where slaves had been sold.

The Dutch, Danish, British, and French also began to bring European salt to Africa. This greatly damaged the Sahara trade, for salt was almost the only product that the Sudan had to offer.

Changes in the Routes.   As a result of these changes, the focus of the Sahara began to shift to the east. The ancient Timbuktu-Fez route and fabled gold trade began to lose importance. The actual shape of the route changed, as well. Sijilmasa had once been the northernmost trading center on that route. But that city decayed and was finally destroyed in the late 1700s. No one city replaced Sijilmasa. Instead, traffic from the northern end of the Taghaza route branched out in several directions.

The ancient caravan center of Walata was also bypassed, with traffic from Taodeni heading almost due south to Timbuktu. Two other routes from the northeast met at In Salah and crossed the Sahara. Each of these three routes passed through Arawan, which became a new important trading center.

Timbuktu. The image of Timbuktu, the fabled city of gold, still attracted foreigners. Many northern Europeans headed there and some societies even offered prizes to the first modern European travelers who could visit Timbuktu and live to tell the tale. More than one explored died trying. In the early 1800s, a British explorer, Alexander Gordon Laing, did reach Timbuktu. But on his return trip, he was murdered and all his journals were burned. A few years later, a young Frenchman, Rene Caillie, did make the round trip—but at great personal cost. His face was badly scarred by scurvy, and his spine was damaged when he was thrown from a camel.

Timbuktu was already in decline by this point, and Caillie talked about his disillusionment when he returned to Europe.

> I had formed a totally different idea of the grandeur and wealth of Timbuktu. The city presented, at first view, nothing but a mass of ill-looking houses, built of earth.

Trade had been the life-blood of Timbuktu. When this declined, the city was in trouble, as Caillie explained:

> From the tower I had an extensive view of an immense plain of white sand, on which nothing grows except a few stunted shrubs, and where the uniformity of the picture is only broken here and there by some scattered hills or banks of sand. I could not help contemplating with astonishment the extraordinary city before me, created solely by the wants of commerce and destitute of every resource except what its accidental position as a place of exchange affords.

EAST SAHARA ROUTES

The Tunis Route. To the east, two other routes were becoming more important by the 19th century. One went from Tunis in modern Tunisia to Kano. Kano was the main center of the Hausa people. This eastward route may have been as old as the Taghaza route but for centuries had not been nearly as much used. Sahara historian E. L. Bovill described how one could tell the age of the route: "Where it passes over rocky ground the deeply worn tracks prove its antiquity [old age] and the great weight of traffic it carried."

In more modern times, Kano became a great trading city, far more so than Timbuktu. Unlike Timbuktu, which survived on trade alone, Kano fostered industries, such as agriculture and textiles. Its inhabitants traded their fine cloth to Europe and in return received silk from France and glass beads from Venice.

The Tripoli Route and the Slave Trade.

The other main north-south route ran from Tripoli to the land of the Bornu around Lake Chad. In many ways, this was the most easily traveled route, but it was not used very often, because it was highly vulnerable to raids. It only became a major road with the rise of the Bornu in the 17th century.

The Tripoli Route relied most heavily on the slave trade. As horrified European explorers described, the route was lined with human skeletons. These were mostly of young women and girls, often clustered near wells that they had died trying to reach.

The slaves traded in West African ports were usually headed for the Americas. But slaves along the Tripoli Route were headed for

By the mid-19th century, Kano had long since replaced Timbuktu as the main trading center on the Sahara caravan routes. (New York Public Library)

the Moslem world. Their destinations were mainly Turkey, Egypt, or the Barbary States (the modern countries of Tunisia, Algeria, and Morocco).

In the early 19th century, the British and other European countries outlawed the slave trade. This ended a great injustice to West Africa, where much of the European and United States slave trade had flourished. It also ended all but very light trade on the Fez-Timbuktu route.

But in the central Sahara, slave trading continued for far longer. On one route, between Wadai in the south and Benghazi in the north, slave caravans were still crossing the Sahara as late as 1911.

The eastern Sudan was a prime center for the slave trade, until the British ended it. (From J.E. Ritchie, *The Pictorial Edition of the Life and Discoveries of David Livingston*)

MODERN TIMES

Colonial Competition. By the end of the 19th century, European states were competing heavily with one another for control of Africa and Asia. In Africa, the European nations managed to colonize most of the continent. Most of West Africa had been taken over by France. The French brought great changes to this region as their power grew. As the Sahara trade had declined, the nomads of the desert had grown poorer. Now the nomads were gradually brought under governmental control.

Before the French, the nomads had often raided caravans, stealing trade goods or animals. Now the former desert raiders were recruited into the Sahara Camel Corps, founded in 1902 to control the desert peoples. The French Foreign Legion was also used to keep the desert peoples under control.

The Automobile. Another great change to the Sahara was brought by the automobile. The automobile's speed meant that people no longer had to depend on the old routes which went from oasis to oasis. The automobile allowed them to make faster journeys and to carry as much water as they needed. The flat, waterless, gravel plains that were so difficult and deadly to caravans traveling on foot proved to be perfect for modern highways. As a result, under French influence, new routes were carved across the Sahara.

In the 20th century, the colonies of West Africa have gradually won their independence from the French, and oil has been discovered in many areas of the northern Sahara, including Libya. Many of the nomads have left their traditional desert homes and gone to work in the oil fields. And many of the oases they once tended are now gradually being swallowed up by the expanding Sahara Desert.

SUGGESTIONS FOR FURTHER READING

Ibn Battuta. *Travels A.D. 1325–1354*, in three vols. (Cambridge: At the University Press, 1958–1971). Hakluyt Society Publications, Second Series. An extraordinary memoir of travels in the 14th-century Islamic world.

Bovill, E. W. *The Golden Trade of the Moors*, second edition (London: Oxford University Press, 1968). A standard history; an updating of the earlier *Caravans of the Old Sahara*.

Brown, Slater. *World of the Desert* (Indianapolis: Bobbs-Merrill, 1963). A generalized discussion.

Gautier, E. F. *Sahara: The Great Desert* (New York: Octagon, 1970). Reprint of 1935 Columbia University Press edition. Translated from the second French edition by Dorothy Ford Mayhew. A classic account of the desert and its life.

July, Robert W. *A History of the African People*, second edition (New York: Scribner's 1974). A very useful general history.

Ross, Michael. *Cross the Great Desert* (London: Gordon & Cremonesi, 1977). A retelling of the experiences of explorer Rene Caillie.

Thomas, Benjamin E. "Trade Routes of Algeria and the Sahara" in *Geography*, volume 8, no. 3, pp. 156–288 (Berkeley: University of California Press, 1957). A useful review, with emphasis on the modern period.

Wellard, James. *The Great Sahara* (New York: Dutton, 1965). A personalized history, stressing modern exploration.

INDEX

Ifrani, al- (Moslem writer) 89
Ihram (Moslem special clothing)
51
Incense 6
Incense Road—*See also*
  Pilgrimage Road
    Abraham and 30–31
    Ancient cities of 34–36
    Arabia and 33–34
    Caravans along 33, 35, 42–45
    Early history of 29–30
    Geography of 30
    Great Desert Route and 30,
      36
    Islam and 40–41
    Map of *31*
    Mecca and 40–41
    Nomads and herders of 30
    Perfume trade of 32–33
    Roman Empire and 36–38
Ipuwer Papyrus (document) 6–7
Iron 9
Irrigation 4, 11, 72
Isaac (biblical character) 55
Ishmael 55
Islam
    Abbasids 46
    Almoravids 78
    Disputes within 46
    Founding of 13
    Growth of 14, 23, 40–41,
      73–74
    Incense Road and 29–30
    Koran and 40
    Mahdi and 24–25
    Mecca pilgrimages 16–18,
      39–41, 53–58
    Mohammed and 39–40
    Nile Route and 1
    Pilgrimage Road and 45–46
    Ramadan 40
    Sahara Route and 77–78, 86
    Shiites 46
    Sudan Route and 17, 23

Sunnis 46
Wahabi movement 58
Isthmus of Suez 18
Ivory 5–6, 8, 23–24, 67, 71

J
Jathrib (city) 40
Jesus Christ (Jesus of Nazareth)
  13, 29
Jewels 33, 83
Jidda (port) 17, 54, 61, 64
Jihad (Holy War) 23, 78
Jordan 30
Judaism 29, 31, 40, 54, 86

K
Ka'bah (Moslem shrine) 39, 45,
  46–47, 53, *54*
Kafuta, Shaykh 'Abjib al- 17
Kairouan (city) 74
Kano (trading center) *94*
Khans (post stations) 49, 51
Khartoum (city) 2–3, 22, 24–25
Koran, The (book) 17, 40, 45
Kordofan Region 9, 12, 22, 24
Kumbi (city) 78
Kush, Kingdom of
    Decline of 12
    Egyptian Empire and 7–8
    Expansion of 9–10
    and Nile exploration 20
    Roman conquest of 11–12

L
Laing, Alexander Gordon 93
Lake Chad 12, 15, 69, 94
Lake Nasser 27
Lake Tana 19
Lawrence of Arabia (Thomas
  Edward Lawrence) 63
Lentils 14
Leo Africanus 80–81, 83, 85–86,
  90

Sunni Moslems 46
Syria 30
Syrian Desert 30

T

Tabari (Arabic writer) 39
Tabuk (city) 50
Tadmekka (trading center) 79
Taghaza (salt mine site) 70,
  74–75, 80–81, 88, 90
Takht-Rawans (decorated litters
  born by camels) *56*
Takruri (African Moslems) 61
Takshif (special messenger) 81
Tana, Lake—*See Lake Tana*
Tatars 50
Tents 4
Thebes 7, 9
Tibesti Region 12, 66
Timber 67, 71
Timbuktu (trading center) 70,
  76, 78–79, 85, 88, 91, 93
Tools 4, 7
Tripoli Route 94–95
Tukrar, Kingdom of 77
Tunis Route 93–94
Turks—*See Ottoman Turks*

Tuthmosis I (Egyptian ruler) 8

V

Vertomannus, Ludovicus 49, 53

W

Wadis 66
Wahab, Muhammad ibn 'Abd al- 58
Wahabi Movement (Islamic
  reform movement) 58, 63
Waid Halfa (city) 25
Walata (trading center) 78, 81,
  88
Wangara (secret source of Arab
  gold) 74
Waterfalls 2, 25
Weapons 7–8, 89
Wells 37
Wheat 14
White Nile—*See Nile River*
World War I (1914-18) 63
World War II (1939-45) 27

Y

Yam, Land of 6
Yasin, Abdullah ibn 78
Yemen 30, 38, 41